JACK McCLINTOCK

THE BOOK OF
DARTS

RANDOM HOUSE
NEW YORK

Library of Congress Cataloging in Publication Data
McClintock, Jack.
 The book of darts.
 1. Darts (Game)   I.   Title.
GV1565.M3   794   76-50077
ISBN 0-394-40805-5
ISBN 0-394-73370-3 (pbk.)

Line drawings by Ivan Powell

Manufactured in the United States of America

9 8 7 6 5 4 3 2

First Edition

THE BOOK OF
DARTS

This is for
NORMA and WARREN MCCLINTOCK
and for
MARY MCCLINTOCK,
who is especially good on the 16s,
and for
everyone who has ever thrown one dart
and found they had to throw another.
And another . . .

AUTHOR'S NOTE

I would like nothing better than to buy a drink for every dart player who helped with this book, but they are so numerous that this would be impossible, and I've bought many of them drinks anyway—after losing dart games to them. The best I can do is thank them all. This book is the product of their knowledge, their skill, and their love of a great game; I just put it together. If there are mistakes that is my responsibility, not theirs.

Among those who were kind enough to explain the game, tell me dart stories and jokes, share hospitality of various kinds, and even, occasionally, allow me to win a game, are David Alderman, Ron Bacchus, Leslie and Stuart Bentler, the late Tom Bertles, Chance Bogert, Di-Ann and Tom Calvin, Ken Cangro, Nancy Clendinen but not Dudley Clendinen (the scoundrel knows why), Dee Curran, Conrad Daniels, Barbara and Scott DeGarmo, Kathy Dobkin, Frank Duffy, Frank Ennis, Pamela Fiori, Ray Fischer, the late Alec Frost, Ken Frost, Jerry Gibbs, Susie and Dr. Pete Gilbert, Don Gold, Paul Gosling, Mike Govlier, Michael Harden, Cyril Hayes, Robin Herman, Tony Heyes, Paul Hong, Michael Hughes, Jim and Kurtie Jackson, Dr. Nancy Beth Jackson, Jan Johnson, Harvey Kay, Tommy Kerr, Harry Kicks, John Koyce, David Krasnoff, Ron Kurtz, Linda Lee, "Art Lessons," Ruth McLeod, Walter Menke, Roger Messer, "Max Mix," Tony Money, Brian Mothersole, Allison and Fred Murray, Adele Nutter, Shay O'Brien, "Orb," Ken Osborne, Mike Palmer, John Parkyn, Neil Raymond, Barbara and Jack Romano, Helen Scheerbaum, Fred Shapiro, Maria Shaw, Bob Theide, Jane Thrift, Barry Twomlow, Nicky Virachkul, Greg Walsh, Vernon White, Miss Doris Williams, Sue and Skip Wilson, Tony Wood, John Yates, Dick Yost, and Charlie Young.

I am especially grateful to Richard Hill for introducing me to the game, to Franklin J. Parisi for singular friendship and practical help, to Louis Donohoe for hospitality in Dublin, to Lorna and Olly Croft for hospitality in London, to Bob McLeod for much time, help, and hospitality in New York, to Tom Fleetwood for telephone aid, to Barbara and Sam Williams for some of the games I have enjoyed most, and to Joe Hitchcock for existing.

And to my literary agent, Knox Burger, a man of rare unclouded vision.

And my editor, Bob Loomis, a gentleman.

CONTENTS

THE BOOK OF
DARTS

1

TONS
THE BOOM IN DARTS

The first time I saw Nicky Virachkul throw a dart was at the
Tripple Inn on Manhattan's West Side, one of those old-fashioned
saloons that have remained in the same neighborhood long
enough to accumulate a few legends and a little character. The
bar area is typically narrow, widening out into a dining room in
the rear with red-checked tablecloths. Apparently by calculation
the room is decorated eclectically— perhaps wittily—with hor-
rendously sleazy Day-Glo posters from the 1960s, stuffed animals

dangling from a wagon-wheel chandelier, and a half-hearted display of artifacts suggesting a vague show-biz connection—publicity shots, unsigned, of various stars, near-stars, and non-stars. Somehow the place manages to rise above all this and manifest a pleasant sort of homely, neighborhood funkiness.

Beside the front door is the dartboard, which is in constant play from noon until about four in the morning when the pub closes. Half the clientele play darts, says the owner Ken Cangro, and on Friday nights you can wait an hour and a half just to get a game. The level of play is so high you'd be lucky to get more than one game a night. A fine $30 dartboard that would last a lifetime in a basement rec room wears out here in six weeks. About a hundred regular players keep their personal darts stacked in boxes behind the bar, each box labeled with a name like Dirty Lil, Rx, Sundance Kid, Captain Numbers, Billy Beercan. It is said that Jane Russell once tossed a few darts in the Tripple Inn, and that on a crowded dart-playing evening some years ago, when *Night of the Iguana* was playing on nearby Broadway, the bartender turned away Tennessee Williams.

The Tripple Inn is a classic darts pub and most of the people there, when not playing darts, are talking about darts. When Nicky Virachkul walked in—it was league night—a parade of players were warming up at the board. A good deal of attention was being paid to Bill Roberson, who is possibly the best black player in the country. A chunky man with goatee and hooded eyes, wearing a white snowman's cap, Roberson throws a fast, mean dart and talks a lot of New Jersey jive in between. Just now he was saying, "Yeah, these meatballs, they think they got a chance? The snowcat kid is gonna give it to 'em." He was throwing so well that the bashful novices arrayed along the bar were saying wisely, "Yes, it's all mind over matter, see."

Then they recognized Nicky and someone said, "Aaaah, why'd *you* have to come?"

Nicky, no smiler, just said a friendly hello and went on passing out black satin vests to his teammates, the Robin Hoods. He was wearing black pants, a white belt, and—though it was January—a short-sleeved shirt. After distributing the vests Nicky went over to the hockey, or throwing line, and the other players melted away. He left his beer on the table. Nicky throws right-handed; for the rest of the night whenever he picked up his wet glass it was always with his left hand.

An hour later, he was again at the hockey and it was game point. People stood around with drinks in their hands and, although the Tripple Inn is a sociable pub and darts the most sociable of games, nobody spoke. There was a smell of tobacco smoke and sour spilled beer; Freddy Fender sang Tex-Mex country-and-western from the jukebox, and a single dart was in Nicky's plump right hand. Two other darts and a burning cigarette were in his left, but everybody's eyes were on the single dart he was psyching himself to throw.

Nicky's dart was typical of a top player's equipment. Made of tungsten, steel, aluminum, and polyester, it weighed 21 grams and was one of a set of three that cost nearly $50, although Nicky hadn't paid for it. Like many tools engineered to do precise tasks the dart was sleek, elegant, pared to essentials, and it had a startling beauty.

All this was too familiar for Nicky himself to be aware of. Besides, he had his mind on something else—the double 16, the shot that would end the game if he made it. If he missed, he could try with the other two darts. Then it would be his opponent's turn, and his opponent was approaching the point where he would be ready to throw for his final double. In the game of 301, the classic English darts game he was playing, you begin the game with 301 points. You must first place a dart in the narrow outer doubles ring. Then you begin to score points, reducing your score to zero—the catch being that the final dart must once again hit a double that brings the score to *exactly* zero. Which is what Nicky, with 32 points left, was hoping to do.

The double 16 measures ⅜″ by 2″ and Nicky was standing eight feet from the board. Throwing accurate darts is more difficult than it looks; most people miss the board completely the first time they try it.

Finally, Nicky threw his dart.

A young man named Mike Govlier, who runs a dart shop in Philadelphia, had once remarked that Nicky's stroke was just like a musical note.

It is. It is virtually perfect enough to seem inevitable. Only his forearm moved, uncoiling snakily out in front of him, a cobra in old Siam, his fingertips snapping open in a delicate *flick* as he let go, the way a snake's tongue will flick out silently. His arm followed through, his body a still platform like the coiled heap of a striking snake.

"There it is," someone said unnecessarily.

Nicky's shiny dart was stuck neatly in the double 16. It must have been one of those Zen throws many athletes know—when you are certain where the missile will end up even before it is released—because Nicky had already turned away to his beer. A few spectators chuckled. Nicky sipped his beer and shook hands with his late opponent, to whom nobody had paid the slightest attention.

Nicky Virachkul was the best darts player in New York City, and the European Darts Organisation ranked him 16th in the world. In 1975 he represented the United States in the World Master's Tournament in England, although when he won his game in the Tripple Inn he had been playing for less than five years. Nicky came to the United States from Thailand in 1968 to study mathematics at Fairleigh Dickinson. He had been a high school javelin champion, which might seem to have been fit preparation for a darts player, but he says the hand-eye coordination required by basketball helped him more. He does not mention it, but his quick mathematical mind is useful too. "Nicky is terrifically bright," says his sponsor. There is something about Nicky's mind—a gambler's mind, perhaps—that makes him very good at certain kinds of play. He has a passionless but fierce concentration of the sort one sees in many top athletes—a tight, pre-occupied intelligence combined with the ability to focus his attention down to an almost abnormally tiny point, in Nicky's case the point of a dart.

A few days after his Tripple Inn game, he was sitting on the customer's side of the bar in Nicky's Place in SoHo, an old bar and grill he owned, with big, gray-grimed windows, a pinball machine called Dipsy Doodle which he regularly vanquishes, and a dartboard over which he presides whenever he can get someone to play him. Behind the bar Harvey Kay was shaking the dice in a plastic coffee cup and proclaiming from the corner of his mouth that he had taught Nicky everything he knows about darts. Perhaps significantly, Harvey Kay does not play darts any more. He just tends bar and plays backgammon, at which his boss has been besting him more and more frequently. It is perhaps only a matter of time before Harvey Kay takes up parcheesi.

There's a theory that you can learn a lot about someone by watching his hands, and watching Nicky's is an education. They are short, pudgy ones, a match to his round face with its secretive Oriental eyes and wispy Fu Manchu. He is not tall, but he is burly and compact, with a round belly, short sturdy arms, an athlete's slim hips. If he were Japanese he would resemble a kind of transistorized sumo wrestler. Yet his hands, unlike the wrestler's groping paws, seldom moved without purpose. He never looked at them. He seemed unconscious that they belonged to him. At rest they were serene and when they moved it was in a spare, pared-down motion. He rolled the dice. He reached for a cigarette from his shirt pocket. The hand left the cup, swung, dipped; there was a brief rustle of the pack, and the hand emerged with the cigarette. It went into his mouth and was lit. No finger had moved a fraction more than it had to. There was no fumbling. The moves were rhythmic, deft, his eyes never left the backgammon board (I doubt that his mind did, either), and probably not one person in a hundred could have found and ignited a cigarette with so little fuss or affectation.

He picked up his backgammon pieces, moved them along the board, scooped up the dice and dropped them into the coffee cup.

"I played an almost perfect game of 501 last night," he said without turning.

"How many darts?"

"Ten." Nine darts is a perfect game in 501, and it is almost never done. I have played darts two years and a good game of 501 for me is around twenty-five darts. "I'm tired," Nicky said. "I played for nine hours."

When I left much later he was still at the bar playing backgammon.

Nicky Virachkul's career neatly parallels the recent burgeoning of darts as a serious sport in America (players insist it is no more a game than golf, which in curious ways it resembles). Bob McLeod, who has had as much to do with that recent spurt of growth as anyone, says, "Darts as the average American knows them is a toy, a game—those little plastic darts and a spun-paper board. But that has zero in common with the sport." The Associated Press recently agreed and included darts, along with ninety-nine other sports, in its official *Sports Almanac*, allotting it six full pages and a photograph. There is even a movement under way, perhaps prematurely, to get darts into the Olympics.

Like the sport, Nicky Virachkul, who is thirty, has come a long way. He has been playing ever since a night in 1972 when, having finished up his part-time bartending job in New York, he walked into a pub called Bananas where there was a dartboard on the wall.

"I just asked a guy to show me how," he says. "I was working until eleven or twelve then, and I'd go into Bananas and play until four. After one or two months I was decent. At eight months I was better than average. I always played better guys, and it cost me money, but that's how to learn. I got used to pressure and the big names that way, and I'm not afraid any more."

Harvey Kay leaned across Nicky's bar one day and said,

"Nicky always did look for people better than he was. I'd go into Bananas and he was the best there. He'd be playing for ten, twenty dollars a game, and it was like a gold mine. I was one of the top four or five shooters in the city then—this was before 60 percent of the people who play now played—and I couldn't find anyone to play me. I found Nicky and he was willing and I beat him easy. He'd only been playing five or six months. I won a lot of money. Yeah, Nicky paid his dues."

Nicky offered a rare grin, but all he said was, "I played a lot."

He still does, and now the darts he plays with are "Nicky Virachkul" signature darts, his name on the box like Henry Aaron's on a baseball bat, and he is paid a royalty on every set sold. He gets his darts free. Accudart sponsors his participation in major tournaments. He promotes darts in exhibitions, for which he is also paid. "I can walk out with a dollar in my pocket and go on the road for a week and when I come back I still have a dollar." Like players such as Conrad Daniels, Ray Fischer, and Bob Theide, who are sponsored by various other dart manufacturers, Nicky is as pampered and respected as any superstar, even though only a few million Americans know his name.

When Nicky started playing in the New York area in 1972 there was a scant handful of dart pubs, no league, and only casual sporadic play. A darter never knew where he could find a game, especially if he was very good. There were a few authentic hustlers around then—before the top players became so widely known through tournaments and publicity—and money play seems to have been more common than it is now, when rising prize money has made legitimate play more profitable. Between 1970 and 1976 the number of serious dart players in America jumped from an estimated 800,000 to over 4 million. By the time Nicky had become an underground superstar in New York, in 1975, there were more than 80 dart pubs in the city with formally organized teams, a lot more pubs with boards on the wall, and a Knickerbocker Darts League with 10 divisions. Washington, D.C., had 96 teams, California had hundreds, and most other big cities were producing dart players at a similar rate, Cleveland and Dallas being especially active. The United States Darting Association formed by Bob McLeod had 23,000 hard-core members—and 20 percent of them were women, a proportion that continues to grow and adds still another attraction to the game for men. Tom Fleetwood in California formed the American Darts Organization whose members are leagues representing thousands of individual pub, club, and team players.

Because the average established darts player probably does not spend much over ten dollars a year on equipment, McLeod is convinced all this growth and activity is in new players. He is convinced enough that the sport is no latter-day hula hoop craze to have invested a great deal of his own money in it, and quit a good executive job. A spokesman for the distillery that sponsors the U.S. Open Darts Tournament says, "Its burgeoning popularity is reminiscent of the bowling fever of the forties and fifties."

This curious phenomenon is occurring not only in the United States but abroad (the United States is "abroad" in a sense; the game originated in England), and darts is very big or growing all over the United Kingdom, Australia, New Zealand, South Africa, Rhodesia (where an ambitious puff adder once slithered into a public house and found itself pinned to the floor by the brass-barreled missile of a quick-thinking dartist), Finland, Norway, Luxembourg, Cyprus, Greenland, Peru, West Germany, Singapore, Sweden (where a new beer has been named "Dart" and sports a dartboard on the label), and of course Japan, where Zen instructors have begun abandoning archery as a medium and using darts. McLeod is always showing off mail orders from some faraway land like Zaire, Cairo, Guatemala, Iran, Gibraltar. Often they come from American embassy or military personnel who have learned the game here or in England, and want to keep their hand in.

In most places organized competition takes place chiefly in taverns and pubs (which to some who would like to see the game grow even faster carries built-in image problems). All over the country bar owners are screwing dartboards to the walls, hanging up a brass lantern or two and a few lengths of Styrofoam "timbers," and declaring, "Now we're a pub." Then they settle back to polish glasses and watch the customers pour in, get intrigued, stay longer, bring more friends when they come back, have more fun, cause less breakage, and spend a lot of money. In five years the number of American pubs equipped with dartboards jumped from about 350 to 7,500, and a lot of them have more than one board—some as many as a dozen. There are more dart pubs in New York now than in Central London.

Dart buffs, having skulked so long in the dim smoky murk of a few ill-frequented saloons, have begun to exult in the names of dart-playing celebrities. They love it when Kojak leans back in his swivel chair, pops in a lollipop, tosses a dart at a "Wanted" poster, and then yells, "*Crockah!*" Or when musician Acker Bilk tells a reporter he always takes his dartboard to parties and plays all alone in another room "to keep me out of trouble" on the road. Or when Sir Laurence Olivier rigs an explosive device in the bull's-eye of his dartboard in *Sleuth*, and hands a set of darts to Michael Caine. Or when the newspapers announce that King Juan Carlos, under the pressure of mounting internal problems in Spain, has taken up darts and installed a board in the Zarzuela Palace. Or when the rock group Steeleye Span decides to launch their sixth album, "Now We Are Six," by staging a dart tournament in the Old Brompton Road—and beats eight other teams from the music industry in the First Annual Steeleye Span Invitational. Or when Tom Jones arrives in Sacramento under cover of darkness in a chauffeured limousine, and Engelbert Humperdinck flies in secretly in a private jet an hour later, and the two play off three legs of darts for the fishing rights on a 3,000-acre ranch they'd purchased. (Jones won, two games to one). Or when Roger Daltry of The Who and "Tommy" tells a gossip magazine he likes to relax by playing darts in his local,

The Kicking Donkey. Or when Jason Robards, Jr., Tammy Grimes, Don McLean, and Kenny Stabler show up at a big dart tournament to throw a few against the champions.

Of course there are thousands of dart lovers nobody ever heard of, some more interesting than others. There's Jesse James, an ex-cop in San Antonio. There's Wild Bill Hickock of Salt Lake City. There's Fred Pleasure, a New York photographer who has collected more than fifty sets of unusual darts since he began playing. There's the bartender who left his job in New Jersey for a new gig at Jakes—"A Saloon with a Touch of Class"—in the fishing village of Stuart, Florida, and brought his dartboard with him. There were those deplorably, if diversely, dogmatic dissenting darts devotees who played on a Spiro Agnew dartboard until a lawsuit resulted (Agnew lost, which took the fun out of it).

In Albany, Oregon, a version of darts is played by lumberjacks throwing double-bitted axes at targets painted on the ends of huge logs, and 100,000 spectators came to a recent annual tournament. Teachers are using dart games to teach arithmetic to slow learners. A rock quartet named itself Tuff Darts, after the player's solacing, if occasionally insincere, comment when an opponent misses. A set of darts and a dartboard went to the moon with the Apollo 11 astronauts.

Companies that have nothing to do with darts have begun enlisting the game's quiet drama in their advertising—Sears was at one time employing tennis, golf, and darts in a TV commercial for the Johnny Miller line of sportswear, and Wishbone salad dressing hired Bob Theide, the popular Pennsauken, N.J., player, to do a TV spot. Dart superstars like Tom Barrett have turned up on television to nip burning cigarettes from Johnny Carson's mouth (astounding Mitzi Gaynor), throw audience-requested doubles with a newspaper covering the board, and toss featherless, sharpened, twentypenny nails more accurately than the average player can throw a dart.

A few years ago there were virtually no important darts tournaments in America. Only one was held in 1970; in 1975 there were a hundred, with competitions held in most major cities. The U.S. Open has a purse of $18,500, the North American Open a purse of $30,000. Conrad Daniels, the number one American player ranked third in the world, estimates that about a quarter of a million dollars in prize money is being played for each year in this country and he believes a fine player could make a full-time living at the game today—perhaps even without gambling.

Like any "quaint" underground cult that begins to emerge, darts has produced its own legends, lore, and myths, its tales of success and failure, tragedy, comedy, and joy, its own characters and superstars. Its world is still small enough for the great names to become known very quickly.

There is Conrad Daniels, the top-ranking United States player who traveled to Leeds, England, to play in the Champion of Champions Tournament as a twenty-to-one long shot—and won. Daniels, who is scientist to McLeod's philosopher, is occasionally described as cocky, although he is not that so much as serenely and disconcertingly confident, with an intimidating coldness of concentration. When not playing, however, he will sit in his Veteran's Tavern in Trenton handing out free darting advice for hours to anyone who troubles to ask. "There are no trade secrets," he says.

There is Bob Theide, perhaps the most popular of American players, who until his accident was ranked fifth in the world and is still spoken of as "the one with charisma, star quality." A strapping, quiet man, he seems genuinely modest to the limited extent that an athlete can be while still maintaining the confidence he needs to win—and perhaps not even that much sometimes. "Even when Bobby was the best, he was never *sure* he was," says a friend of his. But in England a lot of people who watched him play insist he is the best America has yet produced, and one of the first things Bob did when he emerged from his coma was have a dartboard set up in the hospital room and begin throwing from his bed.

There is Ray Fischer of Philadelphia, a clean-cut and gentlemanly fellow who has been a top player for years and shows no sign of becoming less than that; Frank Ennis, "the ambassador of darts" as they call him, who bears a remarkable resemblance to William F. Buckley, Jr., a man of considerable charm who is such a good player he is said never to pick up a dart until it's his turn to throw the first one in a game. There is Al Lippman, "The Iceman," who is said to have turned up in New York dart pubs with his cheap wooden Philadelphia-style Widdie darts and, as a victim puts it, "proceed to blow everybody off the board." There is Dick Yost, a burly former policeman with a manner that mysteriously combines good cheer and a hint of submerged dangerousness, who once played as the "Masked Marvel." He would amble into a strange bar dressed up in a black cape and mask, and inquire innocently, "Who's your local champion?" And Yost's pal Charlie Young who runs a dart pub in a Philadelphia suburb and once beat me in a game by throwing his wooden darts feathers first, and who can talk like a poet about the romance of the dying American version of the game.

Also in Philadelphia is Helen Scheerbaum, the best American woman player. A quiet, matronly grandmother of fifty-three, who gave up her job as a bookkeeper to become a supermarket checker and find more time for darts, she won the 1976 U.S. Open for Women. Helen's roommate is Adele Nutter, a thirty-eight-year-old vision therapist with "better than perfect" eyesight which she says helps her not at all when she plays against Helen.

In California there are scores of fine players, including Javier Gopar, the Mexican-American who is probably the best of them all. He says, "Darts is my full-time interest," and would like to make the game his career.

And there is the inimitable Tex Blackwood who presumably once lived in the Lone Star State before moving to the Northeast. Lean and stringy, Tex continues to walk and talk like a cowboy, wears cowboy hats and boots, and carries his darts in holsters.

He once walked hatless into Jerry's Bar in Philadelphia, his local for years, and nobody recognized him. Tex's specialty is show-biz darts, and he likes to throw from his knees, or over his shoulder, and occasionally while looking into a mirror—although tournament officials have lately leaned toward confiscation of his looking-glass after a Tex-tossed dart neatly buried itself in the floor between a competitor's feet.

"It's a great sport," says Bob McLeod, one of the few philosophers the game has yet produced. "It looks so simple—all you have to do is put that little dart in that little space. But you can't imagine how hard it is, or how magnetizing. It's like eating peanuts." It is so magnetizing, in fact, that one hardly questions the story going around in Philadelphia of the man who began practicing ten or twelve hours a day, "forgot all the other values of a full life," as one observer put it, and is now in bankruptcy proceedings and about to lose his pub. "He also lost a lot of games, which is too bad."

So far darts is chiefly a game for participants, partly because even a bit of watching seems to galvanize the most inert spectator and partly because a spectator must be fairly sophisticated in what to look for in order to enjoy it fully. If you don't know the game, what you want to see is a series of bull's-eyes. A good player can find the bull at will but in most games, most of the time, it is not the best shot to go for. When a good player throws a double 19, then a triple 20, then a double 16, the uneducated observer is likely to shrug and wonder why the crowd has gone wild—the strategy involved, like the darts themselves, having flown right past his head. Even so, spectators are quick to become players, and players who are not yet expert love to watch those who are, and there cannot be anyone who appreciates grace and style and finesse—"good moves"—who would not have a fine time watching Conrad Daniels throw a dart, or for that matter even hearing him talk about it.

Having played the game for over two years without once endangering my amateur status, I've had time to wonder what makes it so attractive to novice and superstar alike; for years it surely wasn't the money. Darts is perhaps the perfect sociable game, played, obviously enough, among friends in a setting that encourages conviviality. A player can concentrate deeply when it is his or her turn—and of what interest is a game that doesn't demand one's best?—yet between throws there is time to relax, chat, smoke a cigarette, sip a drink. It is the sociability quotient that first draws people to where darts is played, and only later to the game itself. "It's a fellowship, a fraternity," says Mike Govlier. "It's social contact," says Tony Heyes, a British transplant who runs a New York pub called The Bells of Hell. "And what is the biggest obstacle in a bar but saying hello? Put your name on the board for a darts game and it's taken care of. You're friends. And after the game, if you didn't like the person all you have to do is say thanks and go back to your drink."

Because darts is a game of coordination and concentration, of grace and delicacy, there is no reason why women—and smaller men—cannot play it as well as big men like Theide.

As for that bit of beer, Scotch, or Irish that usually accompanies a game—many players claim a nip or two has certain beneficial lubricating properties for the wrist and elbow joints, and enhances concentration. Cautiously, they also point out the hazard of lubricating the joints to the extent where one falls down.

Beyond all this is an elaborate constellation of skills one must perfect and which is rewarding when one does; there are errors one must absolutely not make on pain of ruining one's game; as well as a vast gray area of things one has to figure out all alone *and never quite can,* or if one can, cannot ever consistently act on the knowledge. I know, for instance, that there is one particular grip that improves my game some 20 percent when I use it, a certain combination of fingers here and thumb there, a certain amount of tension and pressure on the barrel of the dart. But sometimes I forget, or get impatient to get the throw off, and I miss the shot and know exactly why. The top players are the ones who almost never do that. All this lends the game a richness, a complexity, that is not apparent at first, yet which grows out of its very simplicity. Played for fun, darts is simple. Played for high stakes or in the pressurized atmosphere of a tournament, it can be what Mike Govlier calls it: "The most challenging sport I've ever been involved in. It's *not* relaxing except for the novice. For an Arnold Palmer type, it's very draining emotionally."

"It's just a game of darts," wrote a reporter carried away while covering a tournament, "but you can see the full spectrum of agony and ecstasy on the faces of the shooters."

A player or pub owner can get a complete, high-quality dart outfit—not a toy—for under $50. He can set it up in almost no space at all, and play in any weather in any clothing. He can play the game as intensely as he likes, or as nonchalantly, and take from it commensurate pleasure. He can play alone—there are solitaire games for practice—or in large groups. As there can be little dispute, no referee is necessary. It requires skill and thus provides satisfaction, but the basics of stance, grip, and throw are learned in a half hour.

As others have pointed out, no darts player is asked to perform feats of physical courage, or to get beaten, bashed, or bruised by giants, or to leap and dash about in an undignified manner. No player is required to become wet or cold, or to take a shower with the boys in a smelly locker room, or to go into training, or quit smoking, or remain sober.

The physical benefits of darting do not quite match those of a daily mile run, but it is better for you than watching TV or eating a pound of celery. Says Will Kilkeary, who runs O'Rourke's in Chicago: "I figured in one weekend tournament I went to, counting all the games I played, I transported a total of five tons eight feet, including two and a half tons which I hurled through the air, and I walked a total of twenty-five miles."

Like the bowler or golfer, the dartist is playing essentially against himself. Top players say they don't even think of their opponent or his reputation, don't care what his or her name might be or what he or she looks like or whether he or she is using a heavy dart or a light one, feather flights or plastic flights.

"I'm just shooting my own darts, playing my own game," says Conrad Daniels.

Nobody takes these declarations literally, of course; it strains credulity to imagine that any human being playing a tough opponent in a money tournament can shut his dilemma from his mind completely. On the other hand, watching Lippman, Fischer, Virachkul, Daniels, or Scheerbaum at work on the board, you can almost believe they manage it.

Dart players talk about luck a great deal, and some believe in it, but the fact is luck only helps the novice. For the expert player luck can be said not to exist at all—he never hits a number by good luck; he only mises one through a lapse of talent or concentration. In darts, the thrower has almost total control over what happens. Which, incidentally, is why playing for money is not really gambling.

These simple skills, acquired through so much time and trouble, can be enjoyed in games of exquisite difficulty, of computerish complexity of challenge, of Jamesian psychological devilishness, of arcane arithmetical stratagems and transactional gamesmanship—or in merely throwing a dart for the bull for $100 a pop. Beginners, in a sense, have the opportunity for more fun than the pros, who tend to stick with one or two games. The novice can, and probably even should, practice by playing every game in the book, and many of them, before becoming fixated on beating Nicky Virachkul in 501, invent their own. The dartboard, with its pretty colors and simple geometric shapes, is a diabolically clever piece of design, penalizing every player of the minutest error and offering, in various games, analogues to most of the other sports of modern humankind, from baseball to football, from auto racing to tic-tac-toe.

As in other games that are largely offensive and mainly based on skill, there is lots of room in darts for what Govlier calls "head stuff"—psychological warfare. It is waged constantly, usually subtly, and consciously against one's opponent, often unconsciously against oneself. At times it can become quite harrowing. Daniels remarked once that in golf, which he also plays well, you can spread the tension and paranoia over hours, and dissipate banked frustration with frequent beefy drives. But in darts the tension is distilled into a small physical space and a brief time, and the physical act requires only delicacy and control, never strength, so that enormous pressure is shifted from the body to the mind. If a player loses his touch for a second, he may well lose the game. Darts being a game of millimeters—as baseball is one of inches—it becomes one of painfully tight self-control.

Which is also part of the challenge, of course. It affects every player, some more than others. As McLeod says, "It has something to do with the psychology of mastering something that can't be mastered. In the back of the mind it drives them on, the mystery—why can't I put that little thing in there only eight feet away?"

The flip side of that, the Yang to its Yin, is that sometimes you *can* put that little thing in there, and this is probably the fundamental pull of the game. Now and then, unpredictably, there is a single brilliant moment that comes rarely in life—sometimes in love, work, or games—when the body and the mind, the past and present and future, all suddenly fuse into a strange, seemingly inevitable, unity and clarity—"a stillness inside," as one player poetically tagged it—and even as the missile leaves your fingers you know it will strike precisely where it *must* strike. The way it seemed to happen to Nicky when he threw for the double 16 in the Tripple Inn. It is a moment of utter perfection in a chaotic world, a moment of oneness with the cosmos. Such moments are much too brief and they can't be called up by an act of will; they just happen.

There is a man in Japan, Mr. Ko Ishizaka, who is a Zen darts instructor. Zen has been in Japan for a long time. It has been used for centuries to teach archery, just as archery has been used to teach Zen. But now darts is popular in Japan, and Mr. Ishizaka teaches Zen darts. He says, "You cannot possibly miss that board when your dart flies through the air. The human body is a precise instrument. But there are hundreds of interlocking muscles, and they can exert their utmost power only when there is no unnatural strain anywhere. Allow the muscles to work in harmonious coordination." If you could do that every time, he means, you would always throw a 9-dart game of 501.

"I would have to say that such a thing seems to exist," says John Brodie, quarterback of the Forty-Niners, speaking of the same phenomenon in football. "It's happened to me dozens of times. An intention carries a force, a thought connected with an energy that can stretch itself out in a pass play or a golf shot or a base hit or a thirty-foot jump shot in basketball. I've seen it happen too many times to deny it."

Bob McLeod nods when he hears about this. "Yes. You concentrate so intensely you don't know how it got there. It seems to pop right out of the board."

And I think that is the Peanut Principle—this quasi-spiritual, pseudo-mystical quality that brings people back again and again to any game in which it occurs, hoping it will happen one more time. . . There is something cleansing about it, something cathartic.

This is hifalutin talk about a game, possibly, and most darts players might be embarrassed by it. But there is often—maybe always—more to games than mere play, and more to play than games, and more to both than even players fully know.

Of course there is a Yin to that Yang, too—there always is; that's the name of the game. Hank Burchard, a reporter for the *Washington Post*, walked into a dart pub in the nation's capital, stood around for a while kibitzing, and then asked with gentle irony: "In the end, seen from a distance, taken as a whole, put in perspective, compared with other elements of the grand scheme of things, isn't darts, played with monomaniacal intensity, perhaps a little bit silly?'"

The answer, roared out by one Dick Andrews, a dart player and computer programmer for the Library of Congress, came back fast.

"No!"

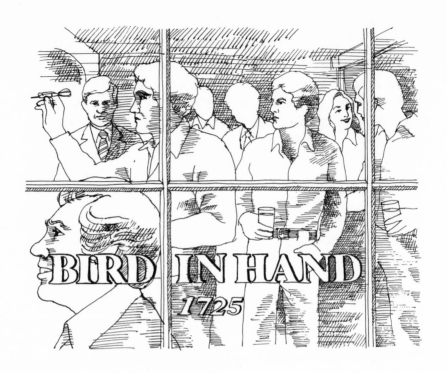

DOUBLE TOP
DARTS IN ENGLAND

John Yates is standing with his nose three inches from the bull's-eye of an elmwood dartboard in The White Horse Tavern in London, and he has a Rothman filter-tip cigarette sticking out of each ear.

Eight feet behind him is the legendary Joe Hitchcock, a year or two over sixty, a tall dapper man with a Menjou mustache, a crisp white broadcloth shirt, and glittering amethyst cuff links. His hair is parted in the middle and slicked back to the sides so that he resembles an Arno character or a classy bartender in a 1930s movie. His blue eyes, despite an evening's prodigious appreciation of Bacardi light, have a clear and serious look. His hands are large, pink, clean, and calm, like a dentist's, and in the right one he is holding an ordinary six-inch carpenter's nail that has been sharpened to an evil-looking point. In his left are five more just like it.

John Yates is the quiet, earnest sort of Texan, not much given to showing off, and he is a bit nervous. He likes Joe Hitchcock, always visits him on trips to London, and admires him extravagantly as a darts wizard. Even so, his knees are twitching.

Joe cocks his right arm and throws the nail at Yates. The nail flips over three times in the air and neatly takes the cigarette from John's right ear. In a flash a second nail has jumped from Joe's left hand to his right and been flung after the first, toward Yates's left ear. The cigarette flips away. The nail hits the dartboard and falls. Yates flinches a distance equal to the length of one nail and turns around with a wan grin.

Hitchcock grins too. Then he throws the other four nails at the dartboard, two into the triple 20 and one into the 20. The fourth bounces off.

"The board's too dry," says Joe. "You need a bristle board for this."

John Yates goes for his beer.

"Very occasionally in every sport a player appears who raises the whole level of play into the realm of Art," wrote T. Finn in *The Watney Book of Pub Games*. "In Darts such a maestro is Mr. Joseph Hitchcock. Is there another man living who can beat champions with a six-inch nail, who can call his score before he throws, who can pin a lighted cigarette to the dartboard, or knock a button from between outstretched fingers? Even if there were, I doubt whether anyone approaches the confidence and grace which Hitchcock brings to these remarkable feats."

Hitchcock himself is not much for claiming greatness. With an instinct for stardom, he allows others to do it for him. "I've never kept check of what I've done," he says, shrugging. "There were other people there and they've got it in books."

The only thing they haven't got in the books is his claim that he once threw a 17-dart game of 1,001—a perfect game. The books say it's never been done. A defunct magazine called *The Dart* once kept check of his games, marathons, and exhibitions for a period of twenty months, and found that Joe's average score per three darts thrown was 71 points—remarkably high. He was billed as The Treble Twenty Wizard because he consistently placed 30 percent of his darts in the triple-20 bed, and The Marathon Marvel because he liked to play games of as many as 25,001 points and never seemed to lose. He was also called The Dean of the Dartboard, which, along with Tom Barrett, is what he still is. You could ask any darts buff in Britain to name the three best players of all time, and Hitchcock's name, along with Tom Barrett's and Jim Pike's, would appear on virtually every list.

Joe has played winning darts with nails, hatpins, knitting needles, and sharpened bicycle spokes. He's beaten virtually every major champion. Yet he has never won a major tournament. Partly this is because he preferred the marathon as a test of the better player to the cut-and-thrust of the —01 games, partly it was because he played exhibitions for pay and was frequently barred, and partly, as he told a surprised Tom Barrett, it was because he had heard he wasn't welcome. He thought other players would refuse to play if Joe Hitchcock played.

But he still can't resist the sight of a cigarette poised in front of a dartboard, and the first thing he had done upon entering the room was nip one from my mouth with a nail, delighting John Yates.

About six years ago he gave it up to run The White Horse, sip Bacardi, and respond to the wishes of "the missus," who had been lonely when he traveled. I went to The White Horse with Yates hoping that Joe could tell me a little of the game's history, but like almost everyone else you talk to, Joe knew very little.

The average player's knowledge of his game extends approximately to the moment he first took it up, and no further. Joe was no different. He remembered buying his first set of darts "at Woolworth's for sixpence in the old money," and that was about it.

Almost nothing is known for certain about the origin and history of darts. Although it is one of the most conspicuous features of British pub life and has been for generations, I could find no indication that any serious writer or historian has ever successfully chronicled the game's past, let alone dealt much with its present. Ron Bacchus, the hardworking publicist for the *News of the World* tournament, once decided to write a brochure on the subject. He made inquiries at a branch library. Two weeks later he received a letter from the main library. It said, in effect: "Dear Mr. Bacchus: We have had an inquiry for information regarding the history of darts, and because you are in a position to know more about it than anyone else, would you be kind enough . . ."

Bacchus, like everyone else, is still in the dark, though he came out of the experience with a good story to tell.

A recent book seemed a promising source: *The Life and Sport of the Inn*, by Michael Brander. But in one hundred and sixty pages it has a total of four sentences on darts, the most illuminating on beginnings being this one: "The true origins of the game seem to be lost in the mists of alehouse smoke."

Tony Wood has also looked into the matter. Wood is a freelance journalist, an editor on a London paper, and editor of *Darts World* magazine. An intelligent, well-dressed young man who wears horn-rims and has the clean-faced look of a new vicar, Wood has pretty much given up the quest. "It's all shrouded in mystery and superstition," he says dryly, after five years of trying. "It just evolved over centuries." Wood has turned his attention instead to assembling a darts museum.

Probably the best story of the game's misty precursor concerns Ethelred II (*"the Unready"*), 968?–1016. Ethelred is said to have been not only unprepared but unprepossessing—so short he could fire a longbow only while lying on his back, an enterprise of poignant pointlessness. He had the idea of throwing cutoff arrows by hand, and encouraged knights to compete with him on his own, so to speak, level. And darts evolved from this.

The only trouble with this enchanting tale is that it is very likely a put-on—no evidence exists to support it.

It takes no linguist or psychologist to suspect that the dart's forebear grew out of man's immemorial primitive urge to throw things at other things and people, and there is the predictable speculation that cavepersons chucked little spears at the pictures on the walls. But for all we truly know they may have played canasta. When you attempt to track darts through the history and literature of England, the word bobs up in one fascinating context or another and then subsides without a trace for years, only to surface later in another context. *The Oxford English Dictionary* finds the word, spelled "darte," as early as 1314 in a reference by the prolific Anon. to "launces, swerdes, and dartes." A mysteriously psuedononymous "Atlas," writing in the 1939 program of the *News of the World* tournament, tells us darts were played in the courts of King Henry II of England (1133–1189), the first of the Plantagenet line, and of Charles VI of France (1368–1422), who was variously known as *"Charles the Well-beloved"* and *"Charles the Mad."* The word recurs throughout succeeding centuries: Coverdale, 1535: "As one shuteth deadley arowes and dartes." Cooper, 1565–73: "A sure and cunning darter . . . a fielde where men exercise darting." Davies, 1662: "They use no other Arms than the Dart, (which they cast . . . dexterously)." Edgeworth, 1820: "He was called Jack the Darter. He threw his darts . . . to an amazing height." (This reminds one of certain latter-day Jack the Darters who also throw to amazing heights, sometimes right over the board.)

But it is clear these are not the same implements Joe Hitchcock bought for sixpence at Woolworth's. They were more likely a form of spear, javelin, pike, or lance used in warfare or practice for it, as suggested by a reference in 1605 by Sylvester:

"Without an aime the Dart-man darts his speare." And a later one by Thirlwall in 1838 to "Archers and dartmen." It seems obvious that the modern dart, as well as the word itself, evolved in some way from these. When spear-throwing died out as a technique of war, it left a perfectly good word dangling in midair to be snatched and stuck onto something else. By then, apparently, there happened to be something on which to stick it—the dart.

The British edition of *The Guinness Book of World Records* states flatly that the game dates from archers' use of heavily weighted, ten-inch throwing arrows for close-in fighting, and it is presumed that around this time darting was practiced as a mere trial of strength, with accuracy being secondary. The objective was to throw the arrows, javelin-style, beyond a certain boundary or to exceed a competitor in distance. A French nobleman in a chronicle of 1530 credits the Irish with being the Hitchcocks of their day: "These Yrishe men darte best, or throw a darte best of all men." And "Atlas," writing in 1938, says the dartes employed by these early Yrishe men weighed a quarter-pound apiece and an expert could hit the bull from twenty-five yards. Apparently, contests of strength had given way to contests of accuracy, bringing darts closer to the game we know today.

One of the few things that is presumed known—since it is recorded over and over again—is that Anne Boleyn in 1532 gave Henry VIII "certain dartes of Biscayne fashion richley ornamented," but nobody recorded anywhere what sort of dartes they were. Although it seems apparent that a dart of some type has frequently been used in war, it was only in the Middle Ages that anything resembling a game developed when the long arrows of English bowmen were adapted for a sport called Butts. Wine butts formed the targets for the new pastime, Finn writes in the Watney book. "The earliest dartboards were marked with wide concentric rings only, and in Scandinavia today such a game is still popular, played with foot-long arrows from a distance of several yards."

DOUBLE TOP

One sensible guess is that in the Middle Ages serfs were required to practice archery several hours daily, else they were fined a chicken or two. But arrows were difficult to manufacture, expensive, and hard to find when shot into the hedge by an inebriated serf (one thing Michael Brander's book does reveal is that Englishmen until a century ago seem to have gone through their entire lives half-in-the-bag from drinking beer all day instead of water). So to sharpen their eyes, the archers devised short arrows that could be thrown by hand. If this was darts' original competitive form, people who love the game today are lucky. Most other games were discouraged as frivolous in those hard-working days, but playing at this was seen as a sort of National Guard meeting. The authorities were pleased. Curiously, Englishmen still often refer to their darts as arrows—or "arrers" —and men you wouldn't otherwise expect to know much of Blake are fond of quoting, usually to their wives, "Bring me my arrows of desire." It's an example of the odd lexicon the game has picked up over the years, constructed and accreted of metaphor, Cockney rhyming slang, modern pub talk, and who knows what else. You can stand baffled in a British pub while the players say things to each other like "muggs away," "bag o' nuts," "fevvers," "Connaught Rangers," and "fried fish." Some of these terms have made the trip to America successfully, but to know the full richness of the argot (see Glossary) you have to hear a Cockney use it.

Those early dartists must have thrown outdoors, at wine casks and the ends of logs with targets painted on them. But English weather being what it is, and the charms of a warm fire and a warm pint of ale being what they are, the players must not have taken long to think of sawing off the end of a log and carrying it inside. People have always wondered where the diabolical clock-face board came from, with its wedge-shaped segments so wickedly numbered, and it may have been around this time that the idea first was hatched. When the slices of log-end began to dry by the fire they would have checked—split radially—as they shrank. This may have suggested a game of superior richness, and when someone added numbers, the end of the concentric target was written on the wall beside the scoreboard. There is no doubt but that the clock-face board has made for a much more varied and interesting game. But its beginnings are lost, and for all we know, Stonehenge may be an elaborate working out of the dartboard's druidic logic.

A young man named Alec Frost, who died years ago in the RAF, wrote a school essay on darts which his mother in North London still treasures. In it, Alec noted what always impresses American players: that darts was played on the *Mayflower* during its historic voyage in 1620. "There are several drawings and paintings showing the Pilgrims playing with steel-pointed shafts of wood with flights," he wrote.

Some, frequently Englishmen, even enjoy connecting darts to the British national character. George Harris of the British Darts Organisation is one of them. He says, "We have learned we can survive by ourselves. We have learned to think and act as individuals, cut off from the rest of Europe. I don't think the Germans would be very good darts players."

Although the game as such was never widely popular in France, certain eighteenth-century prints suggest it may have existed in that country, and Brander, in *The Life and Sport of the Inn*, finds indications of its appearance even earlier, in the seventeenth century. There is a record, he says, of a prisoner in the Bastille converting some metal pins into darts and whiling away the dungeon hours by throwing them at wooden panels. France did play an important ancillary role in the game's history. For many years, well into the twentieth century; many of the darts used by English players were wooden ones manufactured in France. They had H-shaped lead weights mortised into the shaft for balance, and are still being made today.

In his essay on the game's history Tom Barrett says it seems certain that darts has enjoyed its modern form for less than a hundred years, and Brander seems to agree: "Though now common and already well known by 1900, both [darts and indoor quoits] seem to have been of comparatively recent origin." Only very recently have rules and equipment begun to be standardized and even today there are a half-dozen important regional varieties of dartboard, and a plethora of local rules and games. Up and down the British Isles the hockey distance varies from just over seven feet to more than nine.

The first spurt of popularity for modern darts came, Tony Wood thinks, when the public house arrived on the scene in England and games like skittles, quoits, and shove-ha'penny were played widely indoors. Darts seems to have been one of these. The pub itself got its start in mostly poor, rural, or industrial areas where people had little else to do after a long day's labor than visit the public house, not so much simply to drink as for the only human contact they could find outside the church in such communities. Darts was there, and took on the local coloration, and the game has never lost it.

It was a game then, not an industry. For years most players made their own darts, as Tom Barrett later remembered. He learned the game as a boy in the country and first played with rude darts he fashioned of wood wrapped in sheet-lead, with three chicken feathers stuck on the tail. He drew a dartboard on a plank with pencil and compass, and set it up alongside the chicken run. Years later he became the only person to win the *News of the World* finals two years in a row, a distinction he still enjoys.

By the time World War I arrived darts had become so commonplace in English everyday life that pilots immediately thought of using them to bring down German observation balloons, a trick which worked admirably and thus closed the circle of history. Darts, in the form of heavy steel missiles flung by hand from open airplanes, went to war again.

Before the war, however, darts had had to surmount a serious obstacle—that of legitimization under the law. This occurred in 1908, in what must be called a landmark decision in British jurisprudence. The case had everything but sex, and it didn't need that. What happened was that the law, in the form of the Leeds Magistrate's Court, took its first interest in darts since the Middle Ages, and that interest was not benign. The unfortunate upon whom the law's attention fell was one "Foot" Anakin, a publican who possessed, among other distinctions, enormous feet. Foot was accused of presiding over a game of chance on his licensed premises, and haled into court to answer for his sins. Foot, however, was a man of courage and principle and he had his answer ready. He requested the court's permission to show that darts, far from being a game of chance or luck, was a game of considerable skill, and that playing it for a drink or two in a public house was not gambling at all.

The court told Foot to proceed.

Foot got to his feet and galumphed back to his pub, took down his dartboard and three darts, galumphed back, and set up the board in court. Then he stood back eight feet and fired three darts into the triple 20. The triple 20—three of them.

Foot invited the learned and bewigged gentlemen of the court to take a crack at it.

They declined, but ordered a junior clerk to try.

Stepping boldly to the hockey the clerk pitched two darts quite past the board and into the woodwork, and the third a country mile from the 20.

Foot stepped forward and tossed three double 20s.

"Could you do that again, Mr. Anakin?" the magistrate asked.

"Aye," said Foot, and threw three more double 20s—Foot was hot.

The magistrate pondered briefly and threw out the case. Every darts player since then has owed Foot Anakin a debt of gratitude, and it is a pity the man is not better known. Once, just before closing time in a dart pub, I proposed a toast to Foot but not a soul in the place knew his name.

By the time the war ended darts was big enough to require organizing, and in 1924 the National Darts Association was formed to help standardize rules and promote the game—goals identical to those of more recent organizations. The NDA had a kind of slogan: "Darts is the Workingman's Sport," it went. "It is cheap, clean, and skillful."

By the 1930s darts had spread farther and higher than ever before, now penetrating the upper crust where it was played, one suspects, with a touch of condescension (this was the era of "slumming"). King George VI and Queen Elizabeth, now the Queen Mother, even played a game in 1939, in the Slough Social Center, winner tactfully unrecorded. The same year darts found its very own hit song, smashingly titled "The Game of Darts" and sung by The Two Leslies.

The First Golden Age (the second seems on the horizon today) started after World War II. But before that, the game had another obstacle to overcome. This time the problem was not quite so readily resolved and there was no heroic Foot. The year was again 1939, a year in which only one pub in all of England and Scotland was without a dartboard. Clouds of war had gathered and burst in Europe. The world was complicated. And a dispatch from *The New York Times* correspondent in London reported a startling parliamentary crisis. A magistrate's court in Glasgow had suddenly *banned darts*—on the Calvinistic theory that the game encouraged drinking and "n'er-do-wellism."

Such a cry had gone up across the empire that the House of Commons was forced to take notice, and the Chamberlain government was thrown into turmoil.

"The British subject can take appeasement lying down," wrote the correspondent, "but he will not suffer interference with his right to throw darts in precincts where liquid refreshments are dispensed."

When Mr. A. P. Herbert, M.P., stood up in Parliament and asked the Home Secretary, Sir Samuel Hoare, by what authority darts had been banned, Sir Samuel stuck a finger into the blustery gale of public will, and said, in effect, "Actually, none. Muggs away."

And then Sir Samuel allowed that he was quite in agreement with the Royal Commission on Licensing, which encouraged pub games "as a distraction from the mere business of drinking." Dart players shrugged, vindicated, and returned to their games and pints, while the Commons went back to another sticky wicket —trying to work out an alliance with Russia.

But war came, and Tommies took their darts abroad, and Americans stationed in England began to see the game played and eagerly adopted it. (And again the dart itself went to war— or almost did. A Midlands dart team decided darts could be adapted as deadly weapons in hand-to-hand combat, just as they had been centuries before. A good player, they reasoned, could hardly fail to hit a target the size of a dumpling-fed German soldier, while the driver's eye-slit on a Panzer tank was much larger than any triple 20. Woolwich Arsenal thought the team might have something, so they made up a quantity of Explosive Darts Mark I, and tested them on dummies. The darts worked brilliantly—blew the dummies all to bloody hell. Then the ordnance men remembered something: It was most unlikely, they realized, that even the bravest darter could get near enough to an enemy target to be effective with a dart. Not without blowing himself all to bloody hell too. And so with much sentimental regret, no doubt, the project was abandoned.)

It was during and after the war, when dart teams toured England raising money for the cause, that the sport began to attract large audiences and produce authentic folk heroes like Barrett, Pike, Hitchcock, and a score of others. Dart exhibition games were examples of true English culture, and like the music hall, they distracted Englishmen from the pain of war.

When the war ended the *News of the World* tournament started up again and became a kind of World Series of darts that took place every spring and drew over 10,000 spectators every time. But the game reached an apparent saturation point—and stopped. What stopped it, many believe, is what Barry Twomlow, a former NOW champion, calls "the pub stigma." Which is another way of saying "class." The slumming upper-crusters of the 1930s had returned to billiards, balls, and backgammon, and the old-time dart players in the provincial pubs saw their sons shoot a few darts and then go off to London, Manchester, and Birmingham to be factory workers or part of what *Queen* magazine later called "the aristocracy of talent." Some of them at least could scarcely have been seen playing darts, or even inside a dart pub unless taking photographs of it for a slick magazine.

"In the 1920s it was a working-class game," says Barry Twomlow, the big, cheery Northcountryman and former *News of the World* winner who now travels the world promoting Unicorn darts. "It was traditionally played in the pub where if you had sixpence in your pocket you'd go and have a few drinks." Roger Messer says, "There's a tradition of amateurism in England that is difficult to change. It's still largely a cloth-cap game in Britain, with a spit-and-sawdust image. Darts is played where they sell beer, not spirits only. In the West End of London it's not so strong; people don't actually live there except a few of the very rich. But in outer postal zones like Lewisham it is very strong. It's very popular in all the industrial areas, least popular in the stockbroker belt of expensive houses and pubs where someone can buy a smoked salmon sandwich or a good meal" (and where Messer himself lives, and relaxes by playing squash).

One night in a London tippling house I had a clearer insight into the English darts culture. I had found a game with a little man named Ben, who looked exactly like Andy Capp. He seemed to be having a very good time and I asked him what he liked about darts. He said that among his friends the game functioned as the married man's second night out. He gets one night for a pint or two with the boys, Ben said, and then he joins a dart team and gets a second night out—for healthful athletics.

At latest count there were 62,500 pubs in England—an incredible profusion of alehouses, tippling spots, lounges, bars, saloons, and taverns. There are so many and they are so different from one another that there is a Pub Information Center in Vic-

DARTS IN ENGLAND

toria with a 24-hour Dial-A-Pub telephone service (828-3261) that can tell a visitor where to go if he wants history, go-go girls, select food, jazz, a singles spot, rock music, country music, vaudeville turns, drag shows, riverside pubs, market pubs, stockbroker pubs, dancing pubs, writers-and-artists' hangouts, pubs with folksingers, or pubs with darts. Over half of them all have dartboards, though, and a recent national competition attracted entrants from nearly every one.

Pubs and darts are a fully fledged industry in England and enormous sums of money change hands because of the combination. I went to a league match with Olly and Lorna Croft at a pub called The Spurs, whose sign depicted a white rooster with a soccer ball under its wing. In one corner was a little stage with a dartboard mounted on it, brilliantly lit between two white fluted columns. Another half-dozen boards were scattered throughout the room, which was packed solid with people. The bar manager told me that the previous Thursday he had held an impromptu darts tournament instead of hiring a band, and had taken in £163 more than usual—and didn't have to pay the band its £32. The next day, he said, he went out and bought two more dartboards.

Perhaps a £32-a-night band is not much competition, but one estimate suggests that a publican's investment in a darts fixture will add nearly $50 to an evening's take and that, because of darts alone, $14 million a week changes hands during the peak season between September and April.

Nobody argues that darts is not a traditional pub game. But there is disagreement over whether it should remain exclusively that, or grow in other directions. In a slender postwar darts book, Rupert Croft-Cooke takes one side unmistakably: "Darts is no drawing room game . . . it began, and should continue, as a workingman's game. It has no place outside the public house."

Olly Croft, a man of his time, thinks otherwise. He learned to play in a pub, and he's not about to close them down or evict darts. But he has larger dreams.

"What we're trying to get away from is the idea that darts just consists of a lot of little blokes throwing arrows in a boozer."

INTERLUDE

Darts didn't become popular in England merely because it is fun and you can drink while playing. The sport is a perfect microcosm of British humor, courage, competitiveness, character, national pride, social habit, and general eccentricity—all areas in which the English excel. Over the years British journalists, who have the sharpest eyes in the world for the quirkiness of the human animal, have assiduously chronicled dart lore (while ignoring darts as a serious sport unless their paper happened to be sponsoring a tournament) and built a fund of anecdote that illuminates what the game has been like in the nation of its birth.

Henry Cooper drove a lorry for a brewery and loved darts. He played as much as he could, and the only thing in all the world he seemed to love as much was his dog, Ace. He wanted Ace to be with him as he played, and if possible to have as much fun as Henry had. Henry trained Ace to retrieve his darts. Henry would throw three, and Ace would sit back and watch them all go in. Then Ace would get up and trot to the board, leap up and snatch them out one at a time with his teeth, and trot them back to Henry at the hockey. If anyone ever complained about this slight perversion of custom—one traditionally retrieves one's own darts—it is not recorded anywhere. The English love animals.

In 1937, shooting from nine feet, the late Jim Pike played a game of Round the Clock, doubles, retrieving his own darts, in three and a half minutes flat. This means that he hit each double once, in sequence from 1 through 20 plus double bull, taking only ten seconds per successful shot. The record has never been equaled.

In 1952, at Broadcasting Hotel, Birmingham, Jim Pike finished off three games of 301, with no opponent, in two and a half minutes. That record has never been equaled either.

Mrs. Ruth Barrow was ninety-four and regularly playing for the darts team of The Star Inn, Old Heathfield, Sussex. "I will be playing until I can no longer crawl to the start," said the spunky nonegenarian. Mrs. Barrow had played darts for forty years, ever since she won a dartboard in a whist drive.

Walter Gibbs was eighty, blind in one eye, and still winning tournaments a few years ago in Lowestoft, Suffolk. He said, "Playing darts keeps me in contact with young people, which is my way of staying young."

One of the many stunts-for-record the English have devised to keep darts from palling is the ten-hour endurance test—trying to score as many points as possible in ten hours. At last report the record was held by Maurice Steele and Brian Garner of Stoke-on-Trent, Staffordshire, with 327,109 points.

Some estimates claim the average dart is traveling at seventeen miles an hour when it hits the board. Others claim it is traveling at forty miles an hour. It seems apparent that these are more guesses than estimates.

Another of the stunts-for-record darts players have attempted is the endurance game played to 1,000,001 points. Eight hussars of the British Army stationed in Germany established the first record. Scoring at a rate of 28.32 points per second, they reached their goal in nine hours, forty-eight minutes, thirty-one seconds on March 15, 1969. The record stood for years until in November, 1975, a team at The Welcome Inn at Mynyddbach, near Swansea, accomplished the same feat in only seven hours, thirteen minutes, point-four seconds.

Dicky Brett lost his eyesight and both hands in a shell attack in Italy during World War II. Repatriated, he went to the research department at St. Dunstan's Hospital for the Blind with sketches for an apparatus that would allow him to play darts, his favorite sport. The staff were skeptical, but after hours at the drawing board they produced a feasible design, a caliper-like attachment to fit on the stump of his arm, with a steel dart-holder at the end. Dicky Brett plays darts. Because he cannot see, he feels the portion of the board he wants, paces off the distance backward, and throws one. Then his wife tells him where it went. "I can then imagine my next throw," Dicky says.

The 180—three darts thrown into the triple-20 bed earning 180 points—is the dartists' hole in one. As elsewhere, three in a bed is a crowd and difficult to achieve, but worth a celebration. Whenever it is accomplished the cheers go up, and some pubs give free drinks or prizes to the lucky player. Since the slimmer tungsten darts have become popular, and more players have gotten better, the 180 has become a bit more common but it is still an occasion for celebration. Not long ago in the White Bebbs Golf Club, Enfield, two local darts buffs, Billy Lovegrove and Tommy Speller, were playing a game or two of 301. Lovegrove tossed in a 180. When he had calmed down, Speller grinned and told him to leave his darts in the board—all in the triple-20 bed. Then Speller threw all three of *his* darts into the same bed.

It was Joe Hitchcock who raised dart stunting to a level of, if not art, then show business, and he and Tom Barrett are still so admired that their photos are routinely displayed in dart pubs like icons in Greek churches. Joe seems to have mastered every trick possible with darts or dart analogues, and some that seem to go beyond the possible. One was to hit an audience-chosen double while a sheet of newspaper covered the board—shooting blind, as it were. There are a couple of secrets to this trick. One is that if you place the center point of the paper—where the two folds cross and make an X—over the bull as a kind of registration point, it gives an experienced player a fair idea of where the wedges are. And if the stunter misses his double the first time, as he frequently will, then a helper can lift the paper and announce to the audience (and to the stunter) how far off the shot was, and in what direction, so that he has a good chance of modifying his next shot and scoring. Hitchcock says that trick is pretty much a snap. I've tried it and it is not a snap. It is only a snap for Joe Hitchcock. Another player who has watched the cigarette trick closely says it is not "as scary as it seems." Using a dart with large feathers, he says, as the English tend to do, gives the thrower an inch or so of leeway. That does not make the stooge any more comfortable, however.

Probably Hitchcock's finest hour as a stuntman was not witnessed by many people, because it took place in an obscure pub in the provinces.

The principal in the stunt was one Frank Wolfe, founder of *The Dart*. Wolfe was standing around when Joe walked in. Wolfe had apparently thrown and lifted a few the evening before, and he had just asked the landlord for an aspirin and a glass of water. He tells what happened.

"I put the aspirin on my tongue. Joe was standing a few feet away. I stuck my tongue out with the aspirin on it and said, 'Joe, what about that?' He whipped a four-inch nail out of his top pocket and took the aspirin off my tongue clean as a whistle."

As a witness of Joe Hitchcock's performance, I don't question this story at all. The only thing I wonder about is how Frank Wolfe, with an aspirin balanced on his protruding tongue, could have said, "Joe, what about that?" or anything else, for that matter.

* * *

Alex Duff, who is twenty-four, has beaten Barry Twomlow and Alan Evans both. He plays for The Sou'Wester Bar in Glasgow, rated as having the best bar team in Scotland, with five international players on the roster. He has won many doubles tournaments and places consistently high in singles matches. He was a Glasgow area NOW finalist in 1975. If a dart falls to the ground, Duff cannot bend down and pick it up. If one goes too high above the double 20, he cannot reach it. He has had muscular dystrophy from birth, and his arms cannot be straightened to their full length, his hands are always half closed, and his balance is not perfect because he has to walk on his toes.

"Just last week," his brother James says, "he shot six 180s with plenty of witnesses."

Another of the stunts-for-record the English enjoy is time-play—throwing darts until you can't throw another one, much as foolish people once danced in marathons or perched atop flag-poles on one leg. At The Rose and Crown, Perry Wood, North Snelling, Kent, four men played competitive darts in four-hour shifts for 358 hours and eight minutes, nonstop. They played 4,430 games and threw 314,530 darts. They gave the money they raised to the Kent Association for the Blind.

The losers and missers should not be neglected in such a compendium as this. An Australian named Bill Coombs was throwing one day in his local, and he needed a double 20 to go out. He missed it. In fact he missed the board completely and his dart hit the wall above it, dislodging a slab of plaster. The plaster fell to the floor, and when the dust settled Coombs reached into the cavity and pulled out a bagful of gold dust worth two hundred pounds.

Curiously, darts in England did not begin to surge out of its stagnation until about the same time it started growing so fast in America—in the early 1970s. "More happened in the last three years than in the last three hundred," Olly Croft likes to say, and he is not the only one who says it.

The reason for this has partly been an accident of history: certain similar things began to happen simultaneously on both sides of the Atlantic. In Britain, simple inevitable cultural change has a lot to do with it. Because of the nation's dire financial problems of the last few years, what money there is tends to be spent at home, not abroad where the exchange rate is punishing. There is more leisure than ever, and class distinctions are fading. Younger people who once tried to escape their parents' working-class image are now contentedly middle class, and if they ignored the game of darts ten years ago they now feel secure enough to revisit their roots and resume playing. They're finding dartboards in swankier pubs now, too, where they feel comfortable.

That's part of it. The rest of it is people like Olly Croft, David Alderman, Tony Wood, Barry Twomlow, Cyril Hayes, Michael Palmer. B.C.—Before Croft—darts was largely just a pastime, with a phantasmagoria of local rules, local games, local customs, local versions of the dartboard, locally traditional throwing distances, and very little national competition. There wasn't any money. And it wasn't organized. Now, like any self-respecting national sport, darts has at least two major organizations in Britain that claim to represent its interests, and in their different ways both do.

A National Darts Association of Great Britain (NDAGB) was formed in the 1950s and over the next twenty years under a man named John Ross became an unofficial ruling body for the game, influencing the general movement toward standardization of rules. The NDAGB organized leagues, ran local tournaments, encouraged grass-roots dart play, and held a national tournament each year. This was so successful, and so many players were reaching the top classes, that the NDAGB was no longer adequate to their needs. There were only two major national tournaments each year, so that if a player was knocked out early he waited twelve months to play his next big game.

Some players thought the game had more potential. They wanted sponsors and money, darts on the telly, darts crossing oceans, darts in the drawing room. They wanted darts to go respectable.

It was Olly Croft who gave them their wish. A beefy, restless man with wide furry sideburns, he got interested in darts because, as he says, "I'm the sort of bloke who can't stay in a bar and talk for three hours. For something to do I got interested in darts, and *boom*! Within five years I was playing with five dart teams." Just a short time later, he had turned over his business to relatives and was chauffeuring darts players around in the back of his black and gold Bentley sedan.

"Our concern was the top-class player, and giving him top-class play as often as possible," he said.

Croft and others formed the British Darts Organisation (BDO), which now offers a dozen major national tournaments each year, each carrying large cash prizes. He took a group of English dartists to the United States for the first time to play an American team (the Americans won). Largely because of Croft and the BDO, darts is frequently seen on television in England nowadays.

Darts World magazine reported that darts has attracted sponsor money at a faster rate than any other sport in England, joining seven others that receive more than half a million pounds annually. Matches are now booked into West End hotels, and darts is sometimes so respectable that it is almost dull.

Tony Wood thinks the BDO has the right idea, if growth is the goal. "They've shown how to behave. They've got the TV in, they've increased the prize money, they've shown that darts can be presented in a top-mark fashion. The press is taking notice as it never did before."

Paul Gosling, a fine young player, marvels at the changes he's seen. "We wear *uniforms* now! It's just like football, innit?"

Croft says, "Players are getting recognized as artists, as performers, sportsmen, personalities. We can put a darts match on a stage—we've proved it—and hold spectatorship up to eight hours, with a thousand spectators. Tell me another sport that can do that."

Top BDO players, ever concerned about image, even play exhibition games against blind people, who have not stopped playing the national game just because they cannot see. They aim by holding a string tacked to the face of the board, or touch the board and pace off the distance. Some throw remarkably well.

It may be bittersweet that darts could not stay in the pubs forever, but the game was just too attractive. Yet some things seem never to change. There is nothing more pleasant than stopping in at one's local and throwing a few darts, and if there will always be an England, there will always be a pub, a pint, and a dartboard under the inviting glow on the far wall, and always another player waiting to take up the chalks.

William Bernard saw it back in 1947 and doggerelized:

> An Englishman's a man of Parts,
> He likes his beer and game of darts.
> Should anyone his choice deplore,
> 'Twas ever thus for centuries or more.

IVAN POWELL

THE SPIDER
DARTS IN AMERICA

In America there is not one darts tradition, there are two. Until recently these have been quite separate and distinct, with different historical roots, different dartboards, different darts, different games and rules.

One is the game called American darts, which has been played for many years in the coal-mining and working-class regions of Pennsylvania and New Jersey.

The other is the game most of this book is about—English darts.

American darts is dying; English darts is spreading. Until a few years ago many players of American darts had never so much as heard of English darts, but when they did, and when they began playing, darts in America changed almost overnight. The American players brought a competitiveness and a high standard of play that made them almost heroic figures on the darts scene. And they found in English darts an enticing combination: It was a game more sophisticated and challenging than their own, there was tournament money to be won, and players who, for the most part, they could defeat handily since they had been throwing darts for years while English darts in America was relatively new.

The origin of the American darts game is shrouded in mystery and superstition, just like that of English darts in England. The game's history is all oral, based on living memories and tales handed down from player to player. Since the games themselves are all metaphorical variations of the game of baseball, however, it seems likely they were invented in this country, not imported. In Philadelphia, a stronghold even now of American darts, there are those who knew men who were old during World War II who said *they* remembered the game from boyhood. American darts must therefore go back at least to the 1880s. It became quite popular following the war with members of the "52-20 Club"— veterans who were given twenty weeks' severance pay for each fifty-two they had served in the armed forces, and used the cash to finance their readjustment to civilian life by hanging out in taverns. Socially, the game was a mirror image of English darts in England. If you played American darts you probably wore a blue collar or none, you probably worked with your hands, you may or may not have finished high school, you probably preferred beer, blends, and boilermakers to gin or Scotch, and you played the game in a tavern—traditionally the place of male bonding and machismo.

The man who brought American darts and English darts together is Charlie Young.

Charlie Young runs a tavern, The Manor Bar, which is sandwiched between used car lots in the Philadelphia suburb of Frankford, and on the Saturday when I stopped in he was perched on a case of Ortleib's drinking a glass of beer. He got up and shook hands, a tall, dark-haired, friendly man with an open, innocent grin. He drew fresh beers, sat back down, and when he started to talk about the game of American darts I thought for a moment he would burst into tears. "This game is very romantic," he said. "I miss those old days of running from pub to pub. For me, it has memories . . ."

Charlie is said to be one of the dozen top players in the United States—of both American and English darts—and I asked him to throw a few. He said, "Well, we play a game sometimes—it's not really a game, it's just knocking a dime off the top of the board."

"A dime?"

"Uh-huh." Charlie dug a dime from his pocket and laid it carefully on the board's upper rim so that the edge faced outward. He stepped back to the hockey with three light, wooden American-style darts in his hand, and threw one. Its point missed the dime but the wooden barrel jiggled it, and it slid a half inch. His second dart knocked the dime flying.

Charlie looked disappointed. He had clearly wanted to do the trick properly. Shaking his head, he went off for more beer and I threw at the dime, with little confidence and less success, until he came back.

The board hung on a wall behind the oval bar. It was made of pale chunks of laminated wood, end-grain facing outward, and like the English board it was eighteen inches in diameter. The wedges were the same, with the same numbering, but the American board has a very thin triples ring at the outside of the playing circle, and a wider doubles ring adjoining it just inside. The whole interior of the wedge portion is the singles area, with an inch-diameter bull in the middle. Charlie's board had a ragged, two-inch, doughnut-shaped hole pierced clear through it all around the replaceable bull. "I've had this one about four years," he said.

The wooden darts—Widdies, made in Philadelphia—were sticking into the board. Charlie plucked them out and handed them over. The points were extremely sharp, much sharper than those on most metal-barreled English darts. Charlie said the metal darts do not stick well in the wooden board, but the Widdies, thrown with an easy, gentle motion, prick in delicately and stay there.

"Well, *usually* they stay," Charlie grinned. "Sometimes we dip the point in a shot glass of beer to make them stickier. Some guys carry a potato with them and stick the point into it before they throw."

Widdie darts are lighter than metal darts too, varying from 9 to 13 grams. They are sold by the dozen and furnished to players by the bar, which customarily owns them. Because the darts are porous, American darts players are fastidious about moisture on their hands from beer glasses. They feel it soaks into the wood, makes it sticky, and alters the dart's throwing characteristics.

There are other differences. The American board is mounted two inches lower than the English board's five feet eight inches from floor to bull—and the throwing distance is nine inches nearer, about seven feet three inches.

There are dozens of games, Charlie Young said, all of them based on a baseball theme. The wedges are called "innings." Players begin by throwing a dart for the bull, the closer choosing the game to be played. The simplest game is called Everything Counts. The cork winner designates any innings he likes, in sequence or at random, and the players throw in turn for those. Points are earned in this way: 1 for a single, 2 for a double, and 3 for a triple. The number of the inning has nothing to do with the score one earns throwing at it: the largest number of points possible on any throw of three darts is 9.

Charlie and I played a game using the innings 1 through 9— his choice since he had hit the bull. From seven feet three inches the board looked large enough—larger than ever—but the triples ring was so narrow it all but vanished, although Charlie seemed to see it well enough. He was throwing his darts feathers foremost just for the hell of it, and he still drove them into the triple as if it were wide as the Jersey Turnpike. He would toss, the dart would turn gently in the air and present its sharp tip onto the board just where he needed it, making a mild *thik* sound.

Even in its numerous variations American darts is a simple game, far less sophisticated than English darts with its complex counting strategies. But it is demanding enough in its own way (that triples ring is *very* thin), and has been played for so long that the best shooters are all but perfect, which sometimes makes them confident enough to play for a good deal of money.

Money matches have always been important in American darts, more so than in English darts, and the gambling is encrusted with a kind of fussy, ritualistic melodrama that, to Charlie Young, is part of the game's romance. It isn't just the game itself, or even the money. It's the clubby fellowship, the shared assumptions, the charm of the forbidden, and the humor. It is folk culture of a depth and fascination to challenge Margaret Mead.

"It would start at maybe five dollars a game and it could end up a hundred," Charlie says. "It was nothing to win a thousand or two thousand on a match. It was funny too. Before a match the players would haggle for an hour or two like little old ladies— what game to play, the throwing line, how much money. Most people would get there early just to hear the haggling. Money matches would sometimes go on for thirty hours. They shoot until somebody quits, goes broke, or exhausts his credit. But there's an unwritten rule that the last game is free; you can play on nothing the last game and try to get your money back."

The usual form of money play, beyond the common drink-and-a-dollar pickup games, was the fifty-one-game freeze-out, or "shootout," in which players or teams went on for as long as it took one side to win twenty-six games and collect the cash. That is not a short time, so in areas where gambling is illegal a secure site is needed: someone's basement or a tavern backroom in a neighborhood where the cops are paid, or indulgent, or sleeping in the alley down the block. I watched a money match in South Phillie at a tavern in a dim neighborhood under the el tracks, neon beer signs glowing weakly in the chilly mist. When a friend and I walked in—a burly man and a tall one, both wearing trench coats—a tableful of people in the rear erupted. Chairs overturned, bills and playing cards were stuffed into pockets. The card game vanished in ten seconds flat, and the darts match didn't begin until we had convinced everyone we were not the police.

Charlie remembers the old days when money matches flourished. Once, he says, two famous Phillie shooters were involved in a match for a great deal of money. These are invented names but Philadelphians will no doubt recognize the story, which is a famous one. Charlie was there. One player, whose name was not Barney, had brought his own potato and set it on the bar in a little dish. Every so often he would spear it with his darts, starching them up for added sticking power. He was playing against a man not named Rex. They threw and drank, game after game and beer after beer, and some hours later Barney's specimen of *Solanum tuberosum* had come to resemble a platter of mashed potatoes with a little skin left in. Barney was winning. Finally, though, he had to visit the men's room. He did so, but when he returned he found that the frustrated Rex had eaten his potato.

Barney was incensed. "That's it," he said. "The game's over." Rex wanted to play; Barney wrathfully declined. His potato was missing, there was no other potato, without a potato he would not play darts. At last Rex, who was hundreds of dollars down and desperate for a comeback, gave in and left the bar. It was four in the morning. Rex walked through the sleeping neighborhood knocking on doors until he roused a householder willing to surrender a potato. The price was never disclosed. Rex came back with the fresh spud, handed it over to Barney, who fondly placed it in the dish and resumed the match. I enjoyed this story so much I forget who won.

Charlie was so gratified by the hilarity it produced that he thought of another one. This happened—Charlie swears it *happened*—at a hyphenated-American club in Philadelphia. Darts in Philadelphia has always had a kind of Andy Capp quality, and the protagonist of this story (an acquaintance of Charlie Young's whose name he didn't reveal) had an irritated, Mrs. Capp-ish wife. The fellow was always down at the club playing darts, sneaking money from the sugar bowl, and the lady sought a solution. She made her way to the club, snatched the club's only set of darts from the board, marched outside and flung them onto the roof. She stalked home.

Her husband decided that his obligation was to go after them. He climbed the drainpipe successfully and found the darts, but he was a little tipsy. Climbing back to earth he lost his grip and fell into the yard, where he was savaged by the watchdog, losing a trouser leg in the process. He snatched the darts from the grass. He scampered wild-eyed over a fence into the neighbor's yard. But the neighbor had heard him out there, all the yelping and snarling, and concluded that a prowler was at large. The neighbor emerged from his house and thrashed the dartist within an inch of his life. Then he called the cops.

They came and took him away covered all over with blood, rue, and humiliation, and minus three darts and a pants leg. At the precinct house he said, "You're not going to believe this."

For a long time they didn't.

In those days the only darts game known in Philadelphia was American darts. But in California and New York English darts was emerging, spreading quietly up and down both coasts. How it grew, and why at that particular time, nobody knows in detail to this day, but it did. The Philadelphians would have found out sooner or later and the process of absorption would have begun then. But ironically it was Charlie Young, who loves American darts so avidly, who introduced the new game in Philadelphia.

"I had The Silver Bar in Kensington [another Philadelphia suburb] then and a guy came back from California and he had this membership card for a darts league, and he showed it to me. And I said. 'Wow! I've been shooting darts all these years and *I've* never had a membership card.' The guy says, 'Yeah, but they play a different game out there. And they all have their own darts.'

"And I thought, '*We* never had our own darts.' So I started thinking about it."

He was still thinking when his acquaintance returned from California. "The guy came in with brass darts. He's unscrewing them and everything, and everybody in the bar was amazed—these metal darts that came apart and everything. We were really surprised. We'd never seen anything like that in Philadelphia. And then the next thing you know we heard of a $2,000 tournament in Culver City, California, and we put a team together, and a beer distributor put up the money to send us out there: Me, Bobby Theide, Dick Yost, John Melvin, Joe Pacchainelli—'Patches,' we call him. And we won the team championship."

It was the first time the Philadelphians had ever played English darts in serious competition.

The English game is to the American game as chess is to checkers. It is more intense, more complex, and more of a head game, a mind game.

"In American darts," says a player of both games, "a good shooter has total command of the board and the novice has no chance. In English darts even the best miss once in a while. Sometimes the player who knows his numbers can beat a better shooter."

Even today, when many American darts players have been into English darts for years, it is a widespread joke that they can't count. They're not used to it, or weren't until recently. Take what happened to Danny Valetto and Tex Blackwood, playing two Canadians in a game of 301. Tex is good, and Danny is said by some to be the best American darts player in Philadelphia. But the game was 301. There are an all-but-infinite number of ways to reach zero from 301, some of them much easier than others, and it takes a highly specialized brain to master the combinations and remember them all. Danny and Tex had 56 points left, and they hadn't quite mastered counting, and what they chose to do was very far down on the probabilities list.

Tex had a single dart left and he said, "Danny, I'll make the double bull [double 25: 50 points] and you make the double 3." Those being two of the most difficult shots on the board. The double bull is tiny, and the double 3 is a narrow horizontal at the bottom of the board.

Tex blithely shot the double bull, and Danny followed with a double 3 on his first dart.

"Just the worst possible way to win," grinned the player telling the story.

Counting was not their only problem when they started playing 301. There was the matter of dart retrieval. Darts in the American game are customarily left in the board for one's opponent to retrieve, and that is what the Philadelphians were accustomed to. In English darts tournaments they were constantly being called back to get their darts. The English board, which is higher and farther away, was not so hard to get used to, and if a player had trouble adapting to the English brass darts he simply went back to Widdies—except that now he had to buy his own.

Most troublesome, perhaps, was the matter of the yips, which frequently afflicted American players switching to English darts. It is a curious malady. What happens is that sometimes, for no apparent reason, a player finds himself standing at the hockey, dart in hand, arm cocked, grip perfect, poised to throw, and blushing furiously—utterly unable to let go of the dart. He will take aim, his arm will shoot out with perfect form—and then he will look and see the dart still in his hand, as if glued there.

"I mean, you can't release the dart," marvels Charlie Young, shivering. "You freeze up. I saw one guy at a tournament take seven minutes to throw one dart."

In spite of the problems of yips and numbers, the good American darts player seems to have less trouble switching to English darts than English darts players have in switching to the American game, and they switched in throngs. The Philadelphia English Darts League grew from 67 to 2,300 members, and things finally reached the point where all a tournament player had to do was announce, "I'm from Phillie," to gain a definite psychological advantage over his opponents from anywhere else.

"Old-time Phillie dart shooters are the best darts players in the world," says Al Lippman, and old-time Phillie dart shooter.

"I've seen a grain of rice with the United States Constitution engraved on it," wrote Stephen Warner, covering a tournament for the *Atlantic Monthly*. "I've seen a 250-page novel without a word in it that contained the letter 'e.' I've seen a man riding a unicycle across a piano wire while juggling a dozen flaming torches and balancing a glass of champagne on his nose. And I've seen the way Ray Fischer and Al Lippman throw darts—if a fly landed on the board, either of them could nail it down with a flick of the wrist."

That's hyperbole: I've seen Ray Fischer throw a 26 when looking for a 180 (though not often), and I doubt that even Lippman would swear he could nail down a fly more than three times out of ten. Still: When Bob McLeod assembled a list of ten top American dart players, four were Philadelphians—Joe Baltadonis, Charlie Young, Frank Ennis, and Ray Fischer; three more were from nearby New Jersey and played American darts for years: Conrad Daniels, Bob Theide, and Ernie Rill. (Virachkul was a New Yorker, Gopar a Southern Californian, and Tony Money, born in England, lived in Cleveland.)

THE SPIDER

When the Philadelphia players learned how good they were in California, they also learned that there was a darts scene in New York—something they, insular until then, hadn't known. Before long, carloads of Philadelphians were pouring in to the city with their ridiculous little wooden darts, fanning out, playing in all the pubs, and having a perfectly gladsome time. Sometimes they'd stay all weekend. They still talk about it. I asked Charlie Young what the attraction of New York was, after all those years of happily playing American darts in Philadelphia.

Young grinned. "Money. To win money without the hassle of watching out for the cops or the Liquor Control Board or the owner of a bar. They were winning a lot of money in New York."

The tradition of money play in Philadelphia had meant hustlers, some of whom wore the mantle proudly, some of whom denied the name. But the few really good ones all knew each other after a while, and none was getting rich back home. When they heard about New York, though . . .

"In the old days it was work," one of them says. "Friday evening I'd leave the house and hit fourteen joints looking for the action. I'd get $50 a night, maybe, but this was when $2 an hour was good money, and you'd have $200 in a weekend, tax free. It starts as a way to supplement your income—your pay is going to support the wife and kids. But then you see where the money is.

"The most I've ever seen won was $2,000 in one night. But that's been after English darts. That changed it. It was so easy it was like stealing. I don't want to quote figures but it was, you know, $2,000 or $3,000 just for a trip up to New York. New York is where I was introduced to big money. I've played twenty-five years and I never really understood big money until I hit New York."

A writer named Jim Quinn learned firsthand how an old-time Philadelphia shooter worked. He was writing a story for the *Philadelphia Inquirer*'s Sunday magazine and had been told that Norm Finley was one of the best. So he went to see Finley, whom he described as having "the abrasive affability of a poor kid from Kensington who has done very well for himself."

As for Finley, he describes Finley as "the Cassius Clay of darts." Finley has been throwing darts since he was seventeen, but he told Quinn: "I don't shoot much now. I'm thirty-two years old, I got a $91,000 bar in the Northeast, I coach a couple of kids' football teams. Darts doesn't mean anything to me . . ."

Jim Quinn was dutifully writing all this down. Finley was talking, but he was also trying to demonstrate a neat dart trick to Quinn at the same time. He had three Widdies, and he was trying to throw them all at once and get three triples—a shot that sounds, and I would have thought was, impossible.

"I used to be able to do this shot one time out of two," he was saying. "*Missed*, I got six. Most guys can't shoot that good one at a time. I'd go into a bar, tell them what I was going to do: 'Listen, you ever seen it done? You pay a dollar to see some fool jump a horse into a swimming pool down at the Steel Pier. *Anybody* can do that. You've never seen anything like this.' I'd finally get the whole bar betting on me.

"Now I just do tournaments," Finley said, still trying for his three triples. "I can get up for them. But look at Boston. I won in a four-man team, but in Boston you don't even get a trophy for four-man teams. You get $40. I went up there Friday night. Saturday 10:00 A.M. to Sunday 1:00 P.M., I shot darts. That's what a tournament's like. Then, we're in the finals. We start shooting ten o'clock Sunday morning. In the meantime, Saturday midnight, we're hungry. But they close Boston down, midnight. We look all over and finally get a chili dog. Somebody breaks into our room while we're gone. Steals everybody's clothes."

Finley sighed and turned to Quinn. "Look, bet me a dollar —two-to-one I can't do this in two shots. Make it more interesting."

Quinn innocently took the bet, and Finley went on talking and throwing.

"Steals everybody's clothes but mine, because they wouldn't fit anybody else. From me they got five bottles of Johnny Walker I brought with me. So I'm in Boston a whole weekend—I get a chili dog, I sightsee in that park they got up there, and I spend $380."

He stopped throwing and turned to Quinn. "You counting that money?"

Quinn said yes, and Finley went on with his tale. "I come home, my wife says, 'You weren't in Boston—where's your trophy if you were?'

"I tell her they don't give you a trophy in Boston. No good."

Just then Finley made the shot. Chattering the whole time, he had laid three darts at once into the section of the American dartboard that counts as a triple.

"I've never seen *that* before," a bystander remarked.

Finley seemed more interested in finishing his tale, though. "I finally have to phone Boston.

"'Hello,' I say, 'Wasn't I there for the tournament? Didn't I win? And don't you not give out trophies? Here, talk to my wife . . .'"

Finley grinned. "You know what you call that?" He pointed to the dartboard.

"No," said Jim Quinn, still distracted by Finley's convoluted anecdote, "what?"

"You call that getting hustled," Finley said, grinning some more. "Gimme my dollar, son."

Now and then you hear about a player making a full-time living as a darts hustler, but seldom by name, and when you get a name and track it down, the fellow is invariably retired. Or so he will tell you. It is doubtful many could succeed at it today. One player, who at one time or another has beaten virtually all the other top players and is continually improving, once tried, and he doubts it too. "I don't know anyone hustling without working to survive. Without a lot of money or a job the pressure is too much. I did it for six months and it didn't work out too well. I didn't throw like I'm capable of throwing. Also, in order to hustle you have to throw bad darts to begin with, and I don't want to. I want to build my reputation. I want to be a champion."

When Dick Yost proclaims darts will never be snatched from the taverns, he is probably right—one hopes so. But the funky old scene is dying out now, the Masked Marvels, the bragging hustlers, the all-night pub crawls in search of a $10 game. Darts is creeping outward into the spiffier pubs, the white-collar places where it is played by people with professions and money and time on their hands. They don't need darts to supplement their incomes; some of them clip coupons. They play for fun, fraternity, the joy of easy combat—maybe they'll bet a drink or two. There are still pickup games between strangers and challenge matches for money between top players and there probably always will be. But there has been a sufficient infusion of money into darts that hustling for a few bucks has come to seem faintly bush league, a bit sleazy if not actually ridiculous. Darts is trying very hard to become a sport, and has almost made it.

Nowadays, those who could expect to make money if they hustled don't have to hustle to make money. They simply enter a tournament.

Thinking about it, Nicky Virachkul almost drools. "I can't wait two or three years. There'll be $100,000 tournaments with $10,000 first prizes. When we get four or five of those a year, some people can just forget about working."

In the early days of darts in America Conrad Daniels lost $60 to a hustler, in one of his first games of English darts. He has not forgotten it, even though he came back to take $1,400 from the same man later. When he won at Leeds, a twenty-to-one underdog, a man who bet on him took home $7,000, a lot more than Daniels did. But now Conrad probably earns as much from darts as any player in America. He plays and wins tournaments, gets an income from endorsements, royalties, and exhibitions—in 1975 it amounted to between $15,000 and $20,000. And like a surprising number of other top players (Yost, Young, Virachkul, Baltadonis, to mention a few) he has a darts pub in his hometown, Trenton.

Why not?

"Whenever I play anywhere now, I draw an audience of twenty-five or thirty people," he says. "In a tavern, that's a substantial addition to the regular business, so I figured why not open one and put the money in my own pocket." So he bought the Veterans Tavern. When I met him he had owned the place less than a year, and grossed between $300 and $400 a month just in the darting equipment he sold, not to mention the beer and wine.

When darts started growing, an entrepreneurial infrastructure grew up with it: importers, distributors, merchandisers, retailers, promotors, sponsors, salespeople. By the early seventies there were enough serious players to interest tournament sponsors, beer and liquor companies being especially enthusiastic.

As Conrad Daniels says: "In no other sport can you say *everybody* drinks—not necessarily a lot, but drinks."

Nobody can say exactly what made darts explode in the early 1970s, but everyone who tries mentions money and Bob McLeod, who found himself playing this odd game one evening in 1968, in an East Side pub, one of a mere half dozen that existed at the time.

"I wasn't hooked right away," he says, "but soon I was playing a couple hours a day and carrying a set of darts wherever I went." He took to practicing at home while watching television, and wore a hole in the carpet eight feet from the dartboard wall.

Nine months later he had quit his job as assistant to the president of a large international construction company, and organized the USDA. He started publishing the first national darts newsletter, *On the Wire*. He opened Darts Unlimited, Ltd., the first all-darts store in Manhattan. Before long he was organizing tournaments.

"It was nothing then. There was no darts scene at all. It was years before you even had eight pubs."

By 1972 he and others had organized the Knickerbocker Darts League—in eight pubs (there are more than ten times as many now). At the store, he began paying himself a living wage, though less than he had earned before. The game grew, and McLeod knew how to draw publicity, and it grew some more, and before long darts stories were turning up in *The New York Times*, *Sports Illustrated*, *True*, and other magazines. It seemed that almost single-handedly he was creating a boom.

Tom Fleetwood came onto the national darts scene a few years after McLeod and he has found admirers too, especially among grass-roots players, since he helped found the American Darts Organization. Fleetwood is an ex-football player who turned to acting and played the bartender on the "High Chapparral" television series. He drives a Cadillac with California plates that read I DART. Years before the USDA and ADO, he helped form the Southern California Darting Association, now one of the largest in the country.

McLeod and Fleetwood have had their differences—they and their organizations *are* different. The ADO is based in California, where Fleetwood lives; the USDA is based in New York, where McLeod lives. The USDA claims some 23,000 individuals as members; the ADO claims league associations, some twenty-two of them representing perhaps 14,000 players. Fleetwood organizes the North American Open, one of the largest tournaments, and McLeod organizes the U.S. Open, the other large one.

Fleetwood, in addition, is a promoter for Sportcraft, which distributes Unicorn equipment, made by one of the two largest dart firms in England. McLeod is the major American distributor for the other big English darts firm, Kwiz.

Fleetwood is a very large man, a Westerner, an extrovert; McLeod is a small man, an Easterner, cheery and charming but quiet, and he keeps his feelings to himself.

Many dartists in America would like to see the two join forces, but they probably never will. Fleetwood says the ADO is doing things for the grass-roots player that the USDA never contemplated: There was a need and the ADO filled it. McLeod says: "If I disagree I don't want to impede their progress, but I certainly want to go in the direction I think proper. I see ways to make darting bigger. My philosophy may be wrong as opposed to Tom's, but why not cover all the bases? Besides, the country's just too goddamned big."

The country is so big that to claim darting bloomed because two men fertilized it with their egos and love of the sport seems too simple, and of course it is. The best they—and others like Charlie Young and Paul Hong and John Yates and Mike Govlier —could do was harness an interest that was latent but already emerging. If there are four million darts players in the United States, the vast majority belong to neither the ADO nor the USDA, and most of them have never heard of Bob and Tom. They belong to small local leagues, or they play in a pub when they feel like it, or in a church basement, or at home. There are dartists who play in three-piece suits when the backgammon tables are filled in classy lounges, and dartists who play shirtless most of the day and night in untidy beer taverns. There are Andy Capps and Jason Robards, Jrs.

"It's okay to play pool with the guys, but it's not like playing darts with the girls," Greg Walsh said one night in The Tripple Inn.

Conrad Daniels says, "Women are the single most important thing in the growth of darts today. In 1971 and 1972 I was on the West Coast. The people there are young, mobile, liberal, not so stuffy as on the East Coast. Darts started growing and when women got interested it doubled the dart population almost overnight. It gave Daddy a chance to get out, and he'd play mixed doubles with Mommy. There were ladies' singles, and good-looking gals brought in guys to watch. The press came to take pictures of the gals. Guys came in to play with the barmaids."

The top male tournament players in the country are still a bit better than the top women, although there aren't many men who can beat Helen Scheerbaum. Women still play in separate tournaments, or in separate "ladies'" events tacked onto the "main" tournaments, but that may be only temporary. There is a movement, led by Helen, Adele Nutter, and Della Fleetwood among others, to increase purses in the women's matches.

Dart players briskly debate why the women have not quite yet matched the men, but the argument seems pretty much to come down to writer Ellen Weber's comment: "The only reason men are better dart players is they spend more time in bars."

In cities, at least, that is changing, and Daniels thinks that in five years there won't be any separate tournaments left.

One afternoon in a New Jersey darts pub I heard two enthusiasts assessing, half seriously, what effect William Colby's testimony on the CIA might have on the darts image. Colby had admitted the Agency spent some $3 million developing something called a "nondiscernible microbioinoculator," an unsavory gizmo which the press immediately dubbed a poison dart-gun. The two enthusiasts were wondering, glasses in hand, whether the word "dart" appearing in the nation's press would encourage the game's growth, or if the rather depressing context in which it appeared would discourage it.

It was all nonsense, of course, as the enthusiasts knew, but people who have something to gain from the continued growth of darts spend a lot of time pondering their futures, and they think it all depends on the game's image.

The USDA says only a quarter of its organized activities take place in pubs, but the pub is where most people see darts played. There is booze at most tournaments. Dartists drink, no doubt about it. Dan Coughlin, a non-dartist covering a tournament, wrote: "If you gave a personality test to 1,000 dart players selected at random you would find every known virtue except one: abstinence."

Booze in America does have certain exploitable connotations, both guilty and comic, and the press is not above employing them as Coughlin did so innocently, later catching hell, no doubt. Why darts people are so quaintly defensive about such an innocent pastime—innocent, yes; all claim to drink moderately—is something of a mystery. Drinks and darts are, as Daniels says, a natural combination, sanctioned by custom and even justified on the pragmatic ground that up to a point it helps the player relax and concentrate.

But it is their image they are worried about.

"If you want a national sport, it's got to look like one. It's like pool. They tried, but it's still pool—not billiards. The booze could make darts another hula hoop."

Not only booze concerns them. At the U.S. Open Bob McLeod instituted darts' first dress code, thinking to improve the image. He even made Norm Finley go change his pants. There were complaints, but McLeod has not changed his mind. In his office one day soon afterward, he pulled out a stack of photographs taken at another tournament. He found the one he was searching for, a truly astounding picture of an extraordinarily fat young man, his hairy shirtless belly drooping over rumpled beltless jeans, long hair trailing down his back, bare feet. He was throwing a dart. In the background of the picture, people were staring.

McLeod: "How can you get a sponsor for that? I'll never be convinced darts can become a major sport until we get it cleaned up."

Well, perhaps. It *was* quite a photograph. But darts has always been a casual sport and there would be something a bit incongruous about requiring, say, a uniform or coat and tie in a game that came to maturity in working-class pubs. Some players cannot throw encumbered by long sleeves, but most are as tidy as anyone could wish. Certainly the game is big enough now that it is not threatened by a slovenly few; like skill and status, sleaziness doesn't rub off on surrounding surfaces. Still, that photo . . .

What dart buffs really want is to see the game televised in America the way it is in England—they want it to become a spectator sport. Perhaps an annual England-America game?

The Market Diner at West 51st Street and the Hudson River in New York has for years been a gathering place for seamen off the ocean liners berthed at the nearby piers. They have been a motley assortment, often boisterous and raw. The rivalry of international sailors pervades the diesel-scented air along the docks. One day in the late fifties, a darts team from the American liner *United States* challenged a team from the *Queen Elizabeth I* to play 301. The match took place at the Market Diner. It was close, but Tex Rozelle tossed a decisive double 17 for the winning game, and by a score of five to four the British found themselves on the short end of an historic struggle. For the first known time since they invented the game, the English had lost an international darts match. The colonial upstarts were elated and although the defeat must have mortified the British, they are said to have taken it well. The match in the Market Diner presaged an international darts competition that, as the game has grown in recent years, has become intense if still, usually, good-natured.

George Harris says it was the self-reliant isolation of the British Isles that produced a nation of fine darts players, and perhaps it was. If so, it may not be unreasonable to speculate that America's frontier individualism as it lingers in the national soul may produce another nation of darting greats. It may already be happening, though the record is inconclusive. In a Market Diner rematch the following year, the British won easily. Americans compete in the *News of the World* finals, but none has yet won it.

Bob McLeod is optimistic: "In four or five years all the best players in the world may come from the United States. Already our best are as good as theirs."

Conrad Daniels judiciously takes a longer view. "We're really just pioneers," he says. "The test of darts in this country will come in the next generation."

MADHOUSE
THE GREATEST
TOURNAMENT OF ALL

Alexandra Palace is an enormous brick pile in North London, surrounded by parkland and parking lots in a residential neighborhood; Londoners affectionately call it the Ally Pally. Gigantic as the building is, fire regulations prohibit occupancy by more than twelve thousand.

These are not always enforced. Every year in the spring the Ally Pally's Great Hall swells to the rafters with tobacco smoke, beer fumes, and the noisy enthusiasm of up to five thousand more human beings than the law ever contemplated, many of them cheerily addled with strong waters and all in a holiday mood. They come to see twelve ordinary men—lorry drivers, dock wallopers, construction workers, mostly—who stand on a little stage as far away as 150 yards (a perspective that diminishes them to the size of matchsticks) and throw invisible darts at a black dot on the wall which on closer examination through the binoculars many spectators bring along turns out to be a dartboard. Of the half million who entered the *News of the World* annual dart tournament and fought it out in the provinces over the last nine months, the twelve are the last ones left. They are presumably the best in the world, and these are the Grand Finals, the championships—the biggest, noisiest, booziest, most exhilarating dart tournament, a legendary tournament, an epic jock opera, the Wimbledon, the Olympics, the Superbowl of darts.

The Englishman's love for darts is hard to exaggerate. Eight million watched the Grand Finals on television the previous year, 1975, a sixth of the country's population. Perhaps ten million are glued to their TV sets this morning in 1976. There are tonier tournaments, more sedate and respectable tournaments, even tournaments offering richer purses. But this is the one every player dreams of winning because it is the one that crowns, or claims to, the champion of the world.

They began streaming in early, pouring across the lawns from the parking lots full of tiny European cars, dozens of them seeming to pop like circus clowns from each little automobile, beginning to sweat already in the unseasonable heat, taking their shirts off, grinning, waving, shoving, shouting. They looked for the blackboard outside on an easel—"darts/Grand Hall" in pink chalk. They poured past it like army ants. On their shoulders they carried cases of beer, in their hands shopping bags of beer, in their hands suitcases of beer.

"God, don't they sell brew inside?"

Mike Palmer shrugged, grinned, "There's normally quite a queue."

The mass of enthusiasts, their uptilted cans reflecting painful slashes of sunlight, narrowed at the doorways and threaded inside the Great Hall, laughs and shouts echoing and footsteps bamming on the plank floor. The Great Hall is vast, bigger than a football field. From one end you can scarcely make out the sex or color, much less the features, of someone standing at the other. Pillars six feet in diameter support the barrel-vaulted ceiling with its sooty greenhouse windows which were already, on this un-air-conditioned 90-degree morning, letting in too much warmth for comfort. Rows of seats were lined up down the middle. Bleachers rose in the rear. Between the pillars was standing room, a lot of it, all filled. People were everywhere, thousands and thousands of them, hot, close-packed, noisy, smelling of smoke and sweat and beer. The walls seemed to move in. The exits seemed too small and too far away. The queue at the bar was ten deep.

At about this time Tony Money was telling McLeod that he couldn't believe he was here. At thirty-one, Tony Money was vice-president of a British chemical firm, and worked in the United States. Born in Cleveland, England, where he learned to play darts in his local pub at eighteen because that is what everyone else did, he had moved four years before to Cleveland, Ohio, where some of the best darts in America is played. In England he had been a district champion; in America he was virtually unknown. It was customary in his district to throw from seven feet, and Money had spent years trying to get used to throwing from the eight feet of American and international competition. For a long time he rarely entered a major tournament. But in his first important one, the U.S. Master's in 1975, he knocked out Conrad Daniels who was representing the United States in the *News of the World* that year. In his second, the 1976 U.S. Open, he beat George Silberzahn, Ernie Rill, and Ray Fischer—and by proxy or implication everyone else. He was as surprised as anyone. He got $2,000, a trophy, a trip for himself and his wife to Europe for two weeks, and the chance to represent America in the Grand Finals. He had never even seen them before except on television.

So here he was this morning all festooned, all bristling, with ironies. Tony Money of the fiduciary monniker who signs his name "Tony $" and looks after finance for his firm; Tony Money of Cleveland, England, now living in Cleveland, Ohio; English-born Tony Money representing America in an English-born sport in England. The night before he had gone to a pub with some other finalists, and while Bill Lennard sat quietly having a drink or two, he and Sid Webb played darts for two hours. They came out about even. Now, this morning, he was surrounded by well-wishers and the curious, a slender man in a Banlon shirt, a bit soft at the middle with executive spread, a bit of double chin, a shock of dark and slightly graying hair falling toward his right eye, an aristocratic nose. Quite uncertain that he deserved all this attention, he signed autographs. Money was enjoying himself tremendously.

The NOW began as a local tournament in London in 1927, sponsored as a circulation-building promotion stunt by one of those gaudy newspapers the English journalist produces with such unabashed gusto, the *News of the World*. At times the same paper has sponsored dance contests, greyhound racing, small-bore rifle competitions, and an annual town crier contest, but darts outlasted them all. Only a thousand players entered that first year but the winner, forty-one-year-old Sammy Stone, a slater, veteran of the Boer War, and father of nine children, got so much nice publicity along with his silver cup that flocks of dartists could hardly wait to challenge him the following year. The tournament grew and kept growing, expanding to the home counties in 1935, Wales in 1936, the rest of England in 1938.

One Marmaduke "Dukey" Breckon took it in 1939, just before competition was suspended for World War II, and held the championship for eight years until play was reinstated. Miss Doris Williams, a pleasant and eminently English maiden lady, now retired to Orpington, Kent, where she cares for her invalid mother, went to work for the NOW while Dukey was working his way up the playoffs and she stayed there for thirty-five years. She never had a title, she was simply known as Miss Williams, The Woman Who Runs the *News of the World* Tournament. She did everything. Returning to work after the war she found the tournament records had been destroyed in the bombing of London, and set about restoring them. She processed hundreds of thousands of entry forms every year—so many players were entering that one year Jim Pike won an area-final against players who, by elimination, had themselves beaten 75,000 other players just to reach Pike, and lose. That was only an area-final. Before long, the man who won the Grand Finals (no woman has yet reached them) was beating indirectly a half million players all over the United Kingdom.

Good players they were, too. In the early years Miss Williams used to award medals to each player who threw a 180 in any match during the playoffs, but there were so many, and metal so dear, she finally had to switch to certificates. (Throwing a 180 is the dartist's hole in one; some pubs still give free drinks to anyone accomplishing it. Probably the man who threw 180 with the greatest aplomb was Henry Barney, and it happened in the Grand Finals. Henry was standing under the lights, on the stage, with thousands watching. His first dart went into the triple 20. His second dart followed it in. Then he got nervous. He stepped back to recover his composure, and fell off the stage with a tremendous crash. He climbed back up and threw a third triple 20.)

Nine months before the 1976 Finals, in virtually every pub, tavern, and workingman's club in the United Kingdom, fanatical dart players had filled out entry forms, drawn up charts of competitors, and begun to play off against one another. There was no entry fee, and any man or woman could play. Each pub would break down its entrants into groups of eight and these would play off against each other to get house winners, who would play off to become area winners representing perhaps a county or two. Most would be knocked out, a few would advance up the ladder. It would go on for the entire nine months and every pub in the land, every provincial newspaper, would be abuzz with news of the latest winner and plastered with charts showing who beat whom and who would play whom next.

When the rules were relaxed in 1973 Sweden and the United States were invited to send their national champions. For the first two years the American entry was "The Iceman" Al Lippman, who said it took him the entire first visit just to get used to the noise of the crowd, and not until his second trip could he concentrate on his darts.

The third time it was Conrad Daniels, who was also astonished. "It isn't anywhere close to the type of tournament we have here in the States. One big difference I found was that the English players were conditioned to very little warm-up. Each man gets to throw just nine darts before the game begins. Another difference was that the people treated us contestants like celebrities. I signed autographs for an hour and a half. On the other hand there was a lot of booing. Many English people apologized for it, but I had been told to expect booing; I understand it's part of the game there."

Despite these attempts to broaden its base the NOW is still chiefly a United Kingdom event, partly because the officials have to be convinced that any entrant is a bona-fide national champion before allowing him to play. There is not always agreement about that. Canada, for example, couldn't make up its mind and wanted to send two entrants. They were turned down. Excellent players from two dozen darts-loving nations do not compete here, for one reason or another. Even in the United States some question whether a single tournament, the U.S. Open, is the best way of selecting a national champion. They think it might be fairer to choose him on a point basis over a year's time, based on performance at six or eight major tournaments.

THE GREATEST TOURNAMENT OF ALL

In any case and in whatever way, the dozen men are chosen and they have turned up here on the Ally Pally stage with ten thousand watching. They've brought their own darts. The same game is always played: 501, no double to start but it is required to finish on a double. Best two of three legs (games) wins. The throwing line is eight feet. Some have complained that the free start—no double required—is not demanding enough for such high-level play, but the sponsor understands this for what it is (partly show business) and points out that the audience prefers a faster game. A winner every few minutes. Keep the electricity crackling. The NOW does that, and over the years each Grand Final has been the source of an authentic British National Hero. Only three men have won the Grand Final twice and, curiously, all of them were named Tom: Gibbons in 1952 and 1958, Reddington in 1955 and 1960, and Barrett, the only one to have taken it two years in succession, in 1964 and 1965.

To someone who has never seen it before the behavior of the NOW audience is quite as fascinating as the play on the stage. The atmosphere is electric with partisan fervor liberated by the highest achievement of the brewer's art. One recent year 10,000 fans consumed 400 gallons of draught beer and 20,000 bottles—plus what they brought with them. The combination of drink, spirit, and national pride (which is far from dead even within the Commonwealth) is positively galvanizing, so much so that some people worry about it.

"You'll see what I mean," said Tony Wood. "It's a frightening experience, so many people so intent on darts. I had a go at them last year [in *Darts World* magazine] and said it was time to make it not a beer-swilling orgy—it could be bad for the game if there were violence. No policemen can have an effect on fifty mad-drunken Welshmen."

Nevertheless, it is these very qualities that lend the NOW its character and make it unique. And Miss Williams isn't worried, sitting there in the front row in a summery print dress thinking about how it has changed. When she came to the NOW in 1938, darts was an old man's sport. Now she couldn't get over how young the players were, and the audience too. The Great Hall had filled, and while every sort was represented, from rambunctious little kids to natty old men with mustaches and pince-nez, most were young men, workingclass young men.

As for the players, Miss Williams was right again. The oldest was Peter Chapman, who won in 1974. At forty-eight he was the gray eminence. Stefan Lord of Sweden was twenty-two, Joe McKay of Scotland twenty-six, Sid Webb of the Midlands twenty-seven. Gordon Bristo of the Eastern Counties, Shay O'Brien of Ireland, Steward McCleary of the North of England, Bob Brown of Yorkshire, and Tony Money were all in their early thirties. The Welshman Leighton Rees, the favorite, was an elderly fellow of thirty-six and the other two, George Champion from the West and Bill Lennard, a Lancashireman, were in their early forties.

Darts World magazine had called it "one of the most impressive lineups of darts talent ever seen."

A few months before, the bookies had rated Leighton Rees of Ynysybwl, Glamorganshire, as a 6-4 favorite, with Bill Lennard, "Mr. Consistency" as he's called, close behind at 2-1. But the odds kept shifting and just before the match Lennard's professionally guessed chances had dropped to 6-1.

They would stand on the stage, the uproar around them on three sides, their backs to the audience, toss a coin to see who threw first, warm up with nine darts and go at it. Tony Money said later there was little chat backstage between the contestants, and a lot of silent, inward focusing of their concentration. After each throw the player would walk to the board and retrieve his darts, then walk back to the hockey. On the way back he would be facing the bulk of 10,000 people, most of whom would be yelling at, for, against, or about him. I sneaked onto the stage at one point and looked out at the sea of open yelling mouths, and all I could think of was Charlie Young's description of the yips.

Of course most of the audience was too far away to see anything but a tiny man moving his arm, so there was a dartboard-shaped electronic scoreboard eight feet in diameter on the stage, with little lights in each segment. The bulbs would light up to show where each dart landed. Two scorekeepers stood beside giant pads of paper, one to keep score for each player, and a red-coated announcer would call out the scores over the PA system. Heaped on tables were trophies and electric razors and television sets—the prizes—and parked beside the stage, the grand prize, a car. Half a dozen television cameras were mounted around the hall, one of them peeking through a hole in the backdrop two feet from the dartboard, so that audiences at home could watch the players' faces.

When Leighton Rees was introduced it triggered something very like a primal scream from thousands of highly charged Welshmen, a quality of uninhibited bedlam I don't think I've ever witnessed before. The Great Hall was suddenly like a vast pinball machine in which every ball and bumper had a mouth and a can of beer. Rees wore a bright red shirt, had a round belly and friendly round face, and he looked confident. He would play Bob Brown. As the coin was being tossed the Welsh enthusiasts sang a song containing no apparent vowels.

Rees won the toss, drawing more yells, and went first. He threw three darts and got a 20 and two 1s—22 points; any second-week player in Atlanta could have done as well. The Welshmen moaned feelingly, a heavy ripple that ran from one end of the Grand Hall to the other, and Roger Messer leaned over to say, "Not a very good start, is it?"

Brown did better but Rees became himself and soon drew well ahead, and inside of three minutes was ready to finish. He threw, and missed his double. "So they *are* human, aren't they?" someone whispered behind me. Brown won the first leg.

But Rees came back and won the second, took firmer command and brought himself down to 76 on the third, then threw a 20, a 16, and a double 20 to win. The crowd leaped up and roared, a sea of sound and a mural collage of open mouths straining in red faces. Rees stepped down, looking comfortable.

Up next were Stefan Lord and McCleary, a young colorful pair all done up in plaid neckties and bright shirts, McCleary in his lucky red tartan tam-o'-shanter. McCleary looked happy, Lord young, eager, and nervous. I thought of what Miss Williams had said about the players' youth, and what Tom Barrett had said about the "big-match temperament"—that it only comes with experience, only to older men, and not always to them. Even Barrett himself had once given up drinking before big matches, imagining it might help improve his game. But his game fell off instead, and he decided two or three brown ales beforehand might be a good thing, a policy he followed ever since "no matter how auspicious the occasion."

I couldn't tell whether Lord or McCleary had found any brown ale, but it seemed Lord was in trouble from the start.

"He's throwing too fast," someone said. "Much too fast."

"He wants to get off the stage. He's young."

"He'll be off quickly enough if he doesn't slow down."

Lord soon took the first leg but McCleary, tartan tam bobbing, was calm and took two, and Lord was finished.

Now and then a player might be allowed to throw a dart in relative silence but in Britain the name of the game is audience participation, and the audience participated vocally. They could feel those darts in their own hands—I knew, because I could too —*they* were up there playing the champions. Many of them, I guessed, had chosen a player whom they all but actually became, and every toss brough cheers, jeers, boos, hisses, claps, stamps, bursts of weird Welsh chants and football songs. They didn't merely cheer when a favorite shot well, or even simply boo when an adversary shot well, they jeered when an adversary shot badly. In between they drank beer, ate pork pies, and smoked cigarettes. What seemed at first a pleasantly civilized grown-up custom, allowing smoking and drinking in a public hall, began to seem much less so as the smoke thickened and the heat rose and the noise increased. Along the sides, where thousands stood, many on carefully stacked tiers of empty beer cans, one young man perched in three-inch platform heels atop a five-pint picnic can, feet neatly together, wavering slightly, drinking from another can the same size. The smoke drifted across his face like moor mist, or smoke from an historic battle.

Joe McKay of Scotland, in a yellow shirt, got a polite cheer. "And his worthy opponent from the United States, Tony Money!"

Boos blossomed, filling the hall with a coarse racket. A few Americans nearby got to their feet and clapped heartily, but it was as if a little man with emphysema were tootling a tin whistle at the foot of a lighthouse foghorn in the middle of a monsoon. The storm was everything.

"We have always tried to foster a sporting atmosphere," Miss Williams said a few days later, as if she had never heard a boo in her life. "We were very much upset when Money was booed."

Money ignored it and threw calmly, American style, turned a bit sideways and leaning. After a few minutes a heavyset Welshman turned to Roger Messer, "All these Americans have a sort of weird throw, don't they, like Daniels?"

Messer just grinned. He never said that Money was English.

Ron Kurtz noticed something else. "Look at him," he chuckled. Messer looked at Money. "He uses $4 Unicorn darts with molded plastic flights," said Kurtz, who manufactures $50 darts in New Jersey. Messer, who is managing director of Kwiz darts in England, laughed aloud. "It makes you want to cry."

But for the first time in this year's Grand Finals a player took his match in two straight legs, and it was Tony Money who did it, weird throw, cheap darts, and all. He went into the quarter finals. When he left the stage the catcalls were subdued.

Beer cans were beginning to pile up around the pillars. At first only a few were there, stacked neatly on the floor. But now cans were heaping up a foot high at the pillars like scree at the bottom of a cliff, each pillar with its own heap, dregs leaking out to puddle on the planks and soak in with a stale beer, taproom reek, mixing with the crumbs of pork pies.

By now the match was an hour old and well into the afternoon. Heat poured in through the ceiling and, trapped, built up in a true greenhouse effect. Smoke lay solid against the glass like soiled cotton wool. Champion had played Chapman, who had won the championship here two years before, and beaten him, which called for more cheers.

Shay O'Brien and Bill Lennard were playing now. The burly O'Brien, in a green polo shirt, threw a neat 180 and was cheered by the Irish contingent led by Louis Donohoe, whose Dublin pub is O'Brien's home turf.

It was Lennard who won, though. He was a quiet, smiling, handsome man, a lorry driver, dressed today in carefully pressed tans and browns: Something about him makes you think "nice guy." He had ended up with a 70, and went out the hard way and made it look easy. Threw for the 20 and missed into the 1. Threw for the 19, hit it and got back on his track. Left with 50, he casually threw his last dart into the double bull.

By two-thirty it was so hot I was awarding dirty looks to anyone who even lit a match (and cringing when I lit one myself). The beer flowed faster, the crowd was noisier and rowdier. No throw was permitted to pass without the audience's opinion being registered. The heaps of cans around the pillars stood nearly waist-high.

Sid Webb, longish hair, Fu Manchu mustache, and jeans, beat baldheaded dockworker Gordon Bristo.

Experimentally, I shut out the roar of the crowd and listened for the sound of opening cans. Looking at the ceiling in concentration, I heard a snap-hiss about every half-second. And I saw pigeons circling in the smoke. "They live up there," Roger Messer told me.

Tony Money's second entrance, to play Champion, is not so strenuously challenged from the floor; it was as if he'd proven himself worthy of a fair chance. He was throwing well, threw a 180 and earned some cheers, but suddenly the match is halted.

For a better view, some spectators have climbed to the top of a roofed indoor shed. The red-coated announcer—I have come to think of him as the ringmaster—drones politely, "Gentlemen, I must tell you that the darts will stop unless those people come down from the top . . . gentlemen, shake a leg."

With 10,000 booers booing, the climbers put on sheepish faces and came down. And Tony Money, for the first time, paused, and turned, and looked out at the crowd. And in that moment, he believed later, he lost the match.

"After that," he said, "I just couldn't seem to hit the double."

It took a while to end, but when it was over Money was out. He left the stage to mild polite applause and came back to where McLeod was sitting in the front row a few feet from the new car Money might have won. Money looked drained just then, deflated, but he managed a stiff upper lip and a fair smile before the autograph seekers mobbed him.

And then Leighton Rees beat Champion, and the final match for the championship would be played between Rees and Lennard, and it was not only for the sake of suspense that there had to be an interval just then.

For the first time the crowd seemed almost a rabble, almost dangerous. Their noise was stupendous. Two shirtless young men reeled and lurched down the center aisle, hugging and screaming with joy and Welsh pride, bashing into chairs along the way. Behind me an American said, "Can you hear McLeod with his dress code say 'You fellas put your shirts on or we'll have to put you out'?"

A dozen more clambered onto the stage carrying banners emblazoned with their favorite's name—Leighton Rees, of course. They screamed. They waved the banners. They waved cans of pale ale. They waved pork pies. They waved, and munched, fat green leeks gripped by the stems. They emitted almost visible exhalations. They stumbled, bellowed, grinned, pranced, belched, stomped, hollered, roared. One bounded to the brink and flexed a muscleman pose for the TV cameras whose operators, however, had gone to the bar and the loo.

Down front a young man held a five-pint beer can to his face with both hands and drank from it like a fat, thirsty baby.

At the pillars the cans piled higher, rolled across the floor, more beer cans than I have ever seen. One rolled farther and a man descending from the bleachers stepped on it. The can rolled, and he fell with a great noise. He got up, rubbed his eyes, absently kicked the can, and tottered into the gents'.

The line in there for the urinals was appalling and some didn't bother to wait, or couldn't.

It got hotter and the interval dragged on. There was a problem with the television equipment. Out there in England all those millions were waiting for the final game, and God only knew what they'd do if they didn't see it. Riot in their own homes? It would take a while to repair, the ringmaster said.

"Dear Mum" read the tattoo on the young man's arm. The arm lifted and he opened the can of beer with his teeth and foamed his face. He grinned and licked. It got hotter. The hotter it got, the faster the cans snapped open, the hotter the beer inside the cans, and the more the foam rained down. The fellow in the three-inch platform heels was still standing on the can as if turned to stone or salt, or trying for a Guinness record.

Lennard and Rees were on the stage now but the television people were not yet ready. Lennard stood smiling with his darts in his hand, the flights brightly emblazoned with a Union Jack. Rees stood beside him, portly in his red shirt, his dart flights a quiet, respectable, eminently restrained and tasteful white. The two men seemed to float on sound, ignoring each other, ignoring the crowd, two men alone and self-contained, concentrating. The throng had moved up close like fans at a rock concert.

A dignified announcement came from the ringmaster: The television problem would be solved in a moment.

Ten feet away a young man with a beer in each fist shouted

into one of those inexplicable sudden silences: "Stuff the television up your arsehole and let's get on with the game!"

I glanced at Leighton Rees. He looked pained and embarrassed. Lennard smiled gallantly.

At the bar they were saying, "Rees will win it. Rees will win it."

On the floor, the same. "Rees will win it."

Lennard stood quietly and smiled some more.

"I am instructed," droned the ringmaster, having plucked the mike from its stand, "that the aisles must be cleared due to County Council fire regulations. I am instructed that the aisles must be cleared before the match continues."

Boos. Nobody takes a step, though a few sway.

"When the game is completed," the ringmaster goes on, "please remember that there are thousands of pounds of equipment here —please do not charge the stage. *Please do not charge the stage.*"

Bob McLeod was worried. The audience was less overtly hostile than in years past, he said, it was more like friendly rivalry now. But the security force consisted of a dozen unarmed old men in blue serge uniforms. They were respected, deferred to, but obviously not much of a barrier to a platoon of burly young drunks. "The room is wide open," McLeod said. "It's nothing like, say, Yankee Stadium where it's partitioned into smaller sections. There's nothing to prevent . . ."

"A stampede?"

"Yes."

There *was* a current of something in the crowd, a kind of appetite there, but I thought McLeod was engaging in the PR man's hyperbole and love of melodrama, and the fastidious man's fussy suspicion of sweaty drunks in large numbers. As is happened, we were both right.

The shouting, stamping, chanting, and screaming never flagged even after the game began. Lennard threw a 75 and Rees followed with an 85, and commotion became hubbub.

Rees threw a 180 and hubbub shot to the most baroque and tumultuous pandemonium imaginable, a riotous uproar—a sensitive applause meter wouldn't have been safe a block away.

"Rees will win it! Rees will win it! Rees will win it!"

"Rees! Rees! *Rees! Rees!* REES! REES!"

Lennard won it.

He threw his final double as calmly as his first practice dart, and cheers bloomed toward the hot sky. Dozens of beer cans flew into the air like middies' caps at an Annapolis graduation, landing who knows where. Someone tossed a pork pie from twelve yards out and scored a neat double 16 on the electronic scoreboard. Noise shook the walls, rattled the fillings in the teeth, savaged the eardrums, forced the very eyes to blink in protest.

The dozen old men moved about quietly, placing their calming hands on the shoulders and backs that seemed to need them most.

But of course the mob did charge the stage.

Only a dozen reached it and only a half-dozen got up on it, and only one managed to reach the players. He gave Leighton Rees a moist embrace before being taken away.

It took an hour to empty the hall. Soccer players kicked empty five-pint cans into the shins of imagined opponents, mostly bystanders, and grinned apology as they flew past. In the loo, postponed necessity filled the place four, five, six to the stall. Floors were awash, the drains and mains strained.

We walked down the block, got into Olly Croft's luxurious, soundproofed, leather-upholstered, black-and-gold Bentley, and glided away into blessed silence.

Someone said, "Did you see the fight?"

A disappointed Rees fan had snatched up a wooden folding chair and, flailing about, drew blood before he was taken into custody. I remembered McLeod's worries, Leighton Rees's embarrassed face, and something Tony Wood had said: "I think it is only the spellbindingly high quality of the darts played that keeps anything serious from happening."

The next day, Sunday, Leighton Rees and Tony Money were on their way to Bristol for another tournament, a leisurely drive through the beautiful English countryside, and the *News of the World* headlined: "Bill drives to the top—and it's so easy!

"In the steamy heat of London's Alexandra Palace, and before a crowd of 10,000 fanatical fans, Manchester's Bill Lennard became the greatest darts player in the world."

The dignified *Times* of London did not mention it at all.

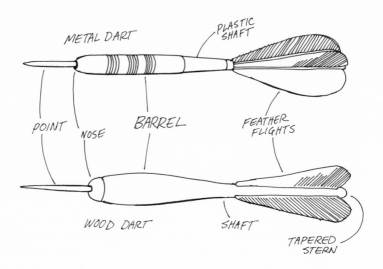

METAL DART

PLASTIC SHAFT

POINT

NOSE

BARREL

FEATHER FLIGHTS

WOOD DART

SHAFT

TAPERED STERN

5

TUFF DARTS
EQUIPMENT AND CHOOSING IT

Bad news: No such thing as a magic dart.

But there is good news too, which is that the dart is a refined, perfected, even elegant instrument, a small triumph of tradition and technology that, better than most, does what it is designed to do and does it very well indeed: It goes where it is thrown. "It would take a wild imagination," says Mr. Tunnicliffe, who manufactures darts in England, "to design a futuristic dart that would be in any way an improvement on the traditional."

The dart is also a rare buy. You can still get a set of professional-quality brass darts with handmade feather flights for between $4 and $7. One player saw a chicly dressed woman in New York's famous Abercrombie and Fitch, looking for a clever gift for her man-who-had-everything, exhibit clear disappointment that the darts cost so little.

Since all you really need to play are darts and a dartboard, and as dartboards cost relatively little too, it would not seem very complicated or expensive to get into the sport. It is not expensive but it can be complicated. Now that there is money to be made in the game manufacturers and designers are scrambling to outdo one another in producing new equipment and fetching accessories.

Beyond the necessities, some of this stuff is useful, some is frivolous, some is convenient, some is a waste of time and money. None is essential. There are for example at least two dart sharpeners on the market, both carborundum, one a cylinder and one a cube, both working on the same principle: You insert the dart point in a cone-shaped hole and kind of stir it around in a circle until it is sharp. These are easier to carry than a length of city sidewalk, but the latter sharpens darts just as well and is a good way to meet people.

It may be nice to have a rubber mat marked with the various throwing distances, but you can achieve the same effect with a little piece of tape on the floor, or a thumbtack, and save some $30. On the other hand, in a casual gameroom where the black rubber tread won't clash with the shag, the mat may add a semi-professional ambience.

Most darts come with a case of some sort, and one is about as convenient as another. But for those to whom self-expression is essential there are scores of boxes, carrying cases, wallets, and pouches, of wood, plastic, leather, and fabric, most costing a few dollars each. More than one dartist keeping his arrows in his shirt pocket has bent over and pronged himself with them, so some sort of protective apparatus is advisable. A simple 25-cent plastic three-hole point-guard will do as well, and give one the funky unpretentious air of caring for the game and not the trappings.

There are little orange discs of finger-grip improver for about 50 cents, there is a thumb-lift wrist-control rig to improve the player's grip and throw for about $2.50. I have never seen a serious player use either.

One should probably begin with the fundamentals; start with the dart.

DARTS

Dart: A pointed missile or weapon thrown by hand; a light spear or javelin; applies to pointed missiles in general, including arrows . . .

A dart is a unity of various elements: darts have parts. These are: point, barrel, shaft or cane, and flights.

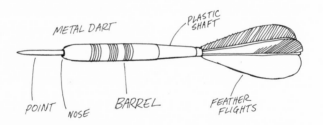

The point of the dart is the point of the dart. It is the point that must be in the face of the board following a throw; any points not there earn no points. Even if the rest of the dart exploded and vaporized on contact, leaving the point in the board, such points would earn points. In fact, operating on this principle, Michael Billson of Oxford, England, who is an artist, cartoonist, dartist, and wit, has been working in his wry British way on an invention he calls the Bumble Bee Mark I. It is a spring-loaded dart with works made from the insides of an old ballpoint pen. When the point hits the board, the barrel and flights "eject." He says it will help the player get more darts in a smaller area, and score higher. "I had thought of incorporating a parachute in the barrel so that when it is ejected it would float gently to the floor," Billson says. "But possibly that would be taking things too far."

Some manufacturers' points are longer than others', and there are players who think the longer points allow closer groupings. Also, if your throw is hard, the short-pointed darts can leave a dent in the face of the board where the nose of the barrel rested. In the long run, this may affect how the board endures.

The barrel is the thick part in the middle of a dart which provides grip, balance, and weight enough to ensure (theoretically) an accurate throw. The point is usually glued into a hole drilled in the nose.

The shaft or cane is like the little stem that holds an ant's thorax to its abdomen, preventing the insect from falling apart inconveniently. In the same way it connects the barrel and flights together and makes the dart a unit. Shafts, skinny little things, do not appear very important, but they are. Their length, shape, weight, and material, and how securely they grip the flights, have a lot to do with the dart's efficiency. Shafts are made of glass fiber, aluminum, plastic, needles, and all sorts of ingenious material. Those of rattan—split bamboo—or willow are called canes. Some have flights affixed, others are slit crosswise at the rear to accept removable flights.

Flights are the feather, paper, or plastic wings on the rear of a dart. Their job is to keep the missile stable in flight so that it flies true, and with the help of the barrel's weight and balance keep the dart's point aimed straight ahead where, presumably, the board is.

There is of course more than one kind of dart, the main ones being wooden darts, brass darts, tungsten darts, variable-weight darts, and custom darts. Each type has special properties.

Wooden Darts

These are the cheapest (under $3 a dozen to pubs) and come in two main varieties. One is the Widdie, which is made in Philadelphia and used in the game of American darts Charlie Young loves so much. They are occasionally used by players who learned the American game first and switched later to English darts, bringing their Widdies along. Widdies are made of light, pale wood, with a lead weight embedded inside and turkey feathers glued on the tapered stern. They weigh between nine and thirteen grams apiece and are handmade; you could spend a day trying to match up a perfect set.

The other common wooden dart is the French dart. These are still made by French peasants in the Jura Mountains and imported into the United Kingdom, where they are much in demand among players around Chester, North Wales, and Manchester. The Japanese, of course, make a replica. The women who make French darts have developed a clever way of mortising the H-shaped weights neatly into the barrels, and it is said that nobody else has discovered quite how they do it. Perhaps no one has tried—it can't be all that difficult, though it is clever. During the past few years the Jura dartmakers have devoted a lot of their time to making chess sets for the tourists, however, and French darts are getting rarer. The price has at least quadrupled.

Brass Darts

Early modern darts were a mere stick with a needle in one end and four feathers stuck on the other, and the old-timers probably threw them with as much skill as Leighton Rees and Conrad Daniels bring to their sleek *objets*, so to speak, *d'art*.

But players wanted an even better dart, "a more effective throwing instrument," as Tony Wood puts it, and they experimented in metal. It was Frank Lowy, a Hungarian patent agent and consulting engineer with offices off Fleet Street, who in 1936 devised that instrument. The primitive darts of the day frustrated

Lowy. The flights would fall out, an annoying distraction, and every dart seemed different. He invented the first precision-made, metal-barreled dart. It was brass, turned on a lathe and then silver-plated. It had a slotted shaft of aluminum with a screw-on cap to prevent falling flights. He called it the Silver Comet.

Lowy engaged a firm of model makers to turn out a few samples and sold them immediately for a total of six pounds. With that as capital he organized a firm called Unicorn, which is now the world's biggest darting equipment company (the entire venture to this day has been financed from that six pounds of seed money). Lowy became a millionaire. Unicorn still makes the Silver Comet.

At its factory in Forest Hill the firm can make a set of darts in a bit over one second, and its marketing division claims a set of Unicorns is sold somewhere in the world every three seconds. Kwiz, the other large English firm, sells nearly as many.

"The advantage of metal darts is control," says Ray Fischer. "They're heavier, and each kind weighs exactly the same."

Because the people who buy them come in an infinite array of sizes, shapes, and aspects, so do darts. With the addition of shafts and flights, there are literally millions of combinations.

Brass darts come in three basic body shapes: straight with the weight evenly distributed throughout, barrel-shaped with the weight at the center, and torpedo-shaped with the weight forward. But those are only the basics. Barrels are grooved, knurled, smooth, or weirdly lumpy, and shaped like bullets, bombs, torpedoes, pencils, teardrops, beer bottles, screwdriver handles, and darts. They are long, short, fat, thin, heavy, light. There are mini-darts (not for official competition) weighing 8 to 11 grams, lightweights from 13 to 19 grams, mediumweights from 20 to 28 grams, heavyweights from 29 to 35 grams, and extra-heavy-weights from 35 to 45 grams.

At one time all professional darts were made in England, and while many American firms have sprung up, some of them producing darts at least as good, most of those sold here are still of

English manufacture. Britain exported some $10 million worth in 1974, doubling the previous year's output, and the growth of the game has been so stupendous that it must at least have doubled again since then. It is a very competitive business, what with two giant firms nearly neck and neck and scores of smaller ones attempting to move in. The dart firms are constantly producing new ideas, a few of which are actual improvements; a few are outright hype. Dart players tend to be conservative and ineffective throwing instruments do not remain on the market for long, but the players are always looking for something new that is also something good—especially after a bad night.

Both Kwiz and Unicorn offer at least a hundred basic brass darts—Kwiz's color brochure is especially dazzling—and both offer signature darts endorsed, and presumably used, by the superstars whose names they bear. Unicorn has Tom Barrett and Tommy Gibbons, both NOW winners, and Kwiz has Alan Evans and Leighton Rees. Fine darts are also made by Tunnicliffe, Paxman, Target, Elkadart, Durro, Trulon, Piranha, and the Dorwin Pencil Co., which hasn't made a pencil in thirty years. In the United States there are Dartronics, Fansteel, Accudart, Eagledart, and others. Some offer rather quirky specialties, such as Tunnicliffe's brass dart with a lead-weighted center, and Elkadart's gold- and silver-plated darts.

Tungsten Darts

Newsbreak from a darts publication: "No league darts player is complete these days without his own private parts [sic] made from tungsten."

Raw tungsten is a dark gray powder, startlingly heavy when poured into the palm. It is more than twice as heavy as brass; its specific gravity is 17 versus 8 for brass. Industrially it is used in balance weights for helicopter rotors, shielding for nuclear submarine reactors, the elements in tungsten arc lamps. Many tennis rackets and golf clubs have small tungsten weights embedded in them to help true their balance.

One day in 1972 an apprentice at the London metals firm of Mathey-Johnson decided, as Tony Wood says, "to make a lovely dart." He worked with tungsten and knew its properties, and realized that the metal could be used to make a dart with the weight of brass (for accuracy) but half as big around. This would mean, he reasoned, that a player could throw much tighter groupings. Thin tungsten darts would not shoulder one another off the mark the way fat brass ones sometimes do.

The apprentice fabricated a prototype, Mathey-Johnson developed tungsten for the manufacture of darts, and the revolution began. There are at least fifty styles of tungsten darts on the market today, all the major manufacturers produce versions, and many—perhaps most—of the top international players use them. In just a few years they have changed the look of the sport.

"It's like skiing or any other leisure activity," says Barry Twomlow. "When the technology improves so that you've got skis that go faster or aeroplanes that fly you more quickly to Switzerland, then the sport gets more popular. It's the same with darts. People don't mind about the cost so much as the performance."

Tungsten darts do perform, and they do cost: between $30 and $60 a set. The price gives pause to a lot of average players (although the lady in Abercrombie's would probably love it). One such player asked Paul Deith, an Associated Press reporter and founder of the Washington, D.C., Area Darting Association, when he should consider moving up from his $4.75 brass darts to $40 tungstens. Deith told him: "When you can take those $4.75 darts and win $40 with them."

There are two reasons for the high price. One is that the metal itself is expensive, about $15 a pound as against 75 cents for brass. The other is that it requires a good deal of hand labor.

Actually, there are two different kinds of "tungsten" darts. Some contain about 90 percent tungsten and cost about $50 a set. Nicky Virachkul uses these. Others, such as those made by Unicorn and Kwiz, are a combination of copper and about 60 percent tungsten, which makes them lighter, but cheaper—about $30 a set. You can tell the difference at a glance; the copper color is visible. Copper-tungsten darts tend to oxidize, which at first was thought to be a disadvantage until players noticed the slight roughening of the barrel gave a firmer grip. Conrad Daniels uses these.

A manufacturer said, "On a cheap [brass] dart if the point is slightly off center we might let it go out; we never would with a tungsten dart." Most of them do seem to exercise more care with their expensive lines, and one small dartmaker, Jim Johnson of England, is so proud of his tungsten darts he has named them Long Jims, Short Jims, Straight Jims, and Plain Jims.

Tungstens may seem to be the ultimate dart (the way brass ones did in the thirties), but they probably aren't. There is already talk of even heavier darts, of more exotic materials—materials like . . . uranium?

Materials like uranium. Uranium is machined as readily as steel and is heavier than tungsten (specific gravity 18.77 versus 17)—the bomb that leveled Hiroshima contained 132 pounds of it in a space the size of a football. And it is available. Tons of spent uranium from nuclear power plants are lying around causing official headaches (and who knows what other maladies), and nobody knows quite what to do with them. Nobody, that is, but Kenneth Seedhouse, who specializes in the industrial use of uranium when he is not playing darts. He thinks we could make darts out of it. Seedhouse concedes that the stuff is both radioactive and toxic, but he claims dartists run an even greater risk from cigarettes and beer than they would from handling uranium darts. He also concedes that this isn't much of an argument, and proposes a uranium core with a thin outer casing of steel or aluminum, or a nickel-plated uranium dart.

So far no path has been beaten to the Seedhouse door by players looking for uranium darts, however. They have tungsten, and it works. "And you don't," says one, "want your bloody hand to fall off, now do you?"

Variable-Weight Darts

At least two of these are on the market, one English and one American. Both of them allow the player to adjust the weight and balance of the dart as he or she likes.

Britain's version is the Reydon, marketed by Fun and Games, Ltd., of Nottingham. With each hollow-barreled dart come ten cadmium-plated lead weights, any number of which can be added or removed by unscrewing a brass nose cone. You even get a ramrod to pack down the plug holding the weights in place. The Reydon comes in three barrel patterns and three weight ranges, each with a ten-gram range of adjustment: light (10-20), medium (15-25), and heavy (23-33). The lighter barrels are made of an alloy, the medium and heavy ones are machined of steel and nickel-plated, threaded for ¼″ shafts. Each dart has seventeen separate components. The set costs about $10 in England.

The American version is called the Variant, made by Accudart and marketed in Britain by Kwiz. Each set comes with 45 separate weights, 15 each of tungsten, brass, and aluminum. They can be used in any combination of either four or five weights per dart. The dart itself has a stainless-steel nose and rear connected by a threaded shaft. You unscrew it, drop any four or five weights onto the shaft, and screw it back together. That gives you 36 combinations of weight—between 12 and 27.5 grams per dart— and over 300 combinations of weight and balance. The weights are different colors, so you can even make pretty patterns. The Variant is threaded for 3/16″ shafts and comes in a handsome mahogany box for about $50.

Obviously, the theory of all this is that the player gets to experiment with different kinds of darts without having to buy new sets every time, and can actually design his own darts. If he wanted to, he could make up three different darts—one for shooting bulls, say, another for the top of the board, and a third for the bottom. It is even conceivable that this might be helpful. I have a set of Variants and people seem to be quite taken with them for about an hour, screwing and unscrewing and losing the weights under the couch, but when the novelty evaporates most end up using brass or tungsten.

Custom Darts

"We are the Savile Row of darts," says Ken Frost.

He was standing behind the counter of his little shop in North London surrounded by his wife, his mother, his son, and a few hundred sets of Frosty's custom darts. His father, Leslie George Frost, the original Frosty, started making handmade darts back in 1926 and his mother sold them down the lane from a little tray around her neck, like a cigarette girl in a pretentious night club. Frosty has carried on the family business and makes several standard handmade darts which he sells over the counter for about $1.50 for brass barrels only or about $3.40 for complete darts. They are cheaper than many mass-produced ones.

But Frosty's specialty is the custom handmade dart and he holds over a thousand patents for individual designs. His pricing policy is unusual. If you want a custom dart—any kind of dart you can dream up—Frosty will make it for you for the same price as a similar standard dart, unless he is forced to buy extra tools for the job. If he does, the price goes up.

A man came in Frosty's one day and showed Ken his right forefinger. The tip was missing. He wanted darts. Frosty devised a set with a deep groove positioned where the stump would rest. The man ordered four sets.

Another man came in and held up his right arm. There was a metal hook, but no hand. Frosty invented a slotted dart that fit onto the tip of the hook in such a way that it released itself when the hook reached a certain point in the man's throw. He is still playing with them.

Another man came in to browse. He couldn't make up his mind; some of the standard darts looked good but there was something just not right about them. Finally he decided what it was. They were backwards. The flights were where the point should be, and vice versa. He picked one out and asked Frosty if he could have it the other way around. Frosty said sure, made up a set just like it only he placed the point where the shaft would have been and drilled out the nose for a shaft. The man loved it. Frosty showed off a prototype. "It throws a bit oddly," he said, "but you get used to it."

He shrugged.

"A custom dart inspires confidence."

FLIGHTS

To understand flights, you've got to understand turkeys. Unfortunately, turkeys are not the most arresting phenomena in the natural world, nor the easiest to understand. They are so stupid that some young ones cannot figure out how to eat, and must be enticed to their food by the addition of colored baubles to catch their attention, and even ancient wise turkeys have gazed up with such rapt astonishment at a rainstorm for so long that their nostrils filled with water and they drowned. Turkeys are therefore difficult to love, but darts players are at least thankful for them and not only on the day set aside for thanksgiving. They give us flights.

The turkey, it is said, is the only bird producing suitable feathers for flights. Furthermore, only a few feathers from each turkey can be used—those from the leading edges of each wing—which requires a lot of turkeys. One manufacturer, Unicorn, imports turkey feathers by the ton (a ton amounting to some 450,000 feathers) and discards about 90 percent of each delivery. Kwiz imports them from the Chicago stockyards, turns them into flights in England, ships them back to the United States where many are bought by Chicago dart players, and still manages to turn a profit.

But there is an ongoing shortage of turkey feathers, the problem being that times are changing, people are changing, and even the turkeys are changing—none of them necessarily for the better. Your classic, traditional turkey was a mottled gray bird weighing twenty-five to thirty pounds, with terrific rigid wing feathers. He was perfect for the big old-fashioned holiday dinner, and ideal for feather flights. Farmers in England used to hand-pluck these fabulous creatures and earn pocket money by saving the feathers for the dart man.

Turkey breeders later instituted mechanical plucking, sometimes with the help of hot oil and water soaks, a process which both leached out the natural oils and mangled the feathers so that not many of them were left in shape for flights. Mechanical plucking was imperfect, too, like the turkey itself, and sometimes a few feathers were left on the bird. When the dressed carcasses were displayed in those little see-through packages, the feathers frequently offended turkey purchasers.

The breeders developed a brand-new turkey. This one was white, with nice pale feathers so the buyer would not notice a few of them left on the bird. Hence the Great White Turkey Changeover. Unfortunately, feathers from white turkeys were not very good for dart flights.

Then the turkey people decided that buyers wanted turkeys with broad breasts and more tender white meat, so they made another new turkey. The new turkey obediently developed a big firm bosom, but at the expense of the strong wings that provided good feathers for flights. Then they found that demand had fallen off for big turkeys, and invented smaller ones. It was the big ones that made good flights.

What with all this, the quality of turkey feathers plummeted, a shortage resulted, and prices went up. Demand for feather flights never lessened, however. Paul Hong, a darts distributor in Boston, says an idea of the demand for fine feather flights can be had from the fact that a California man has gone into the business of fashioning handmade flights from big, old-fashioned turkeys, asking $8 a set for them, wholesale, and getting it. Ordinary ones cost about $3 retail.

Tom Barrett believes there is just nothing like feathers. After all, they were made for flight, if not for flights. But there are other kinds, and each has adherents. Polyester flights are the next most popular: thin plastic flights that fold flat for carrying, unfold for insertion into the X-shaped slits in the rear of shafts designed to hold them. A few players, especially in England, still use paper flights. A few more use molded plastic flights, the same thick and unlovely sort you see on toy-store darts. Like feathers, most of these come in a variety of shapes and sizes.

Beyond these, there are a few genuine oddities. In the early 1970s, because of the turkey-feather shortage, Unicorn was making a kind of corkscrew, bottle-brush-shaped flight of substitute feathers. These worked well with darts under 31 grams and for players with a light throw, although they lacked the lift for use with heavy darts. Elkadart makes a "Clearway" flight of polyester, the standard shape but with the center cut out so that a following dart could pass right through without deflection, or so Elkadart claims. Another flight, made by Benz Ltd. and marketed through Kwiz, had three wings instead of the usual four. Benz says this offered a better view of the board.

When you eavesdrop on serious dart players holding a technical discussion of the virtues of various flights, they sound like a magpie flock of veteran aviators, darting their hands around and chattering of "lift" and "aerodynamic drag." It is very impressive, but a typical absence of unanimity makes it less than helpful for the beginner. Even the combined genius of twentieth-century aeronautical engineering does not enlighten us much. The cover of one dartmaker's brochure carries a photograph, taken at the Department of Aeronautics of the University of London, of a dart in a supersonic wind tunnel, zipping along at a simulated speed of a thousand miles an hour. You can see what appear to be lines of force at the nose and flights, but they don't tell the layman anything.

SHAFTS

What is there to say about shafts? Not much, really. All do the job; most do it reasonably well.

They either have flights affixed, in which case they are discussed under flights, or they have slots in the rear to accept various forms of flights—usually paper or polyester. Aluminum shafts are said to last longer than glass fiber or plastic, but cost a bit more. Some of the rattan and willow canes are designed so that you can remove the adapters, cut them to any length you like, and put them back together. An interesting new shaft has recently come onto the market, the invention of one Russ Schmidt of California. He used four needles, daubed some plastic on the ends, and stuck them into a threaded fitting. They are thin, light, and grip flights well, altogether an admirable backyard tinkerer design.

Shafts are easy to get and cost little ($1–$3) and, again, the best thing is to experiment until you find ones you like.

CHOOSING DARTS

You will have gathered that darting is something less than a science, as well as something more. Even the finest players throw atrocious darts from time to time, and there are very few principles on which they all agree. One of them is that playing with the right dart makes a difference. Of course they do not agree on *how much* of a difference, or on what is the right dart.

There are one or two obvious ways of choosing the wrong dart, however. One is the love-at-first-sight fallacy. Some darts are so attractive that they capture the imagination instantly, like the glance across a crowded room. The result of premature commitment is frequently the same (and for the same reasons): chronic incompatibility. The same is true of the brand-name fallacy. Most of the top dartists have endorsed a certain set of darts for some manufacturer. Ordinarily the player in question actually uses this dart, but it does not mean the same dart is best for someone else, even though it sells a lot of darts. ("The manufacturers love it," grins Daniels. "They get rich.") Players endorsing signature darts are paid a royalty on each set sold, which raises the retail price between thirty cents and a dollar. This is not much, but it is too much when another dart may be even better. Like tennis rackets, darts cannot be chosen well by proxy. Testimony of an expert witness: Having met Bob Theide and admired his game, I bought a set of "Theide" darts and played with them for a year. They are good darts. I played a mediocre and erratic game with them. I switched to another set for a time, and stayed about the same. Now, I have picked out what I am certain is the perfect dart for me, choosing it without regard for brand names or aesthetic considerations. That I remain mediocre in no way neutralizes the argument: I am mediocre in a much more consistent fashion.

The best place to begin choosing a set of darts is in a shop where there are lots of them to try out, and a dartboard on the wall to do it on. Look for a dart that you feel a natural, perhaps even mystical affinity for—love at first sight, even—but then try it, compare it with others, keeping an open mind. Find a dart that feels right in the grip you use, seems to balance truly in the hand, inspires confidence in the mind, and flies well in the air. A dart should fly straight without wobbling or waggling. It should appear to zip across space in a flat trajectory, or float cleanly to the board. The throwing motion is an easy one, and a compatible dart should not make it seem otherwise. The ideal is to discover a dart that is right for your throw, not to try accommodating your throw to some particular dart. You'll have enough trouble without that.

The customary laws of motion apply to the flight of a dart but with such complexity that no one has ever managed to codify them, although a few facts are known—or at least guessed. Weight is the most important consideration, and enlightened opinion seems to line up on the side of heavier darts, especially for beginners. A heavy dart has a satisfying heft in the fingers—

you feel as if you're throwing something. Some, with the balance at one point on the barrel, can be felt the way you would feel a pebble you were trying to boost through a hoop with thumb and forefinger. Heavy darts tend to be more accurate, as slight deviations in the player's throw do not affect them as seriously as they would a lighter dart.

When a dart wobbles in flight, its balance is wrong for your throw, or you have thrown awkwardly, or with a poor grip. If it waggles from side to side, or sticks into the board at a kind of sideways angle, ditto. If it goes into the board nose down with the flight sticking up like the tail of a ground-pecking bird, dart doctors say you may need a longer shaft or flights. One expert feels that darts fly differently in the dense atmosphere of a pub than in an airy tournament hall, and he recommends slightly heavier darts for tourney play.

After a player has become more expert, then a lighter—especially a *thinner*—dart is worth considering. All else being equal, a lighter and thinner dart offers the chance to earn higher scores through tighter groups. Theide's thin brass darts (16-19 grams) have allowed him to place three in the triple 20 and still have room left over for one or two more, a situation in which Tom Barrett's thumping fat bombs would have shouldered each other into an awkward splay. Robin Varian, a fine East Coast player, started with heavy darts and now uses 15-gram darts, and says: "My game has improved every time I switched to a lighter dart." But thinner darts are harder to control, tending to slip and roll in the fingers. They require closer attention to the grip.

As for length, that too depends on the individual player's throw. British players tend to use long darts, Americans shorter ones. Ray Fischer, for instance, uses a very short tungsten. With the secure modesty of the talented, he says: "I *need* a short dart, otherwise I hit myself in the eye." The choice here, then, depends largely on whether the player throws from the eye, the cheek, the ear, the shoulder, or the chest. It also depends on how he holds the dart: Some players begin a throw with the dart held almost vertical, so that length is only important in how the dart actually flies.

Most darts come with flights already attached. Presumably the manufacturer has tried to provide a suitable one, one that will make his dart look good and fly well, and many players are satisfied with what they get. But some are constantly experimenting, and one went so far as to ask for a chart describing the best flight-type for each barrel-type. No such chart exists. Michael Lowy of Unicorn says, "If a dart was shot from a gun, where the impelling force is always the same, it would be possible . . . [but] every dart player has his own personal throwing style, angle of throw, force of throw, and the point at which the dart enters the board varies considerably."

So that in choosing flights, too, the player is alone in a thicket of possibilities. Even polling the top players yields only ambiguity. At a recent U.S. Master's tournament—in progressive, pragmatic America—70 percent of the players used feather flights, versus 16 percent using polyester and 7 percent using either wood darts (with feather flights) or molded plastic flights. But at an England–Wales match I saw, in which most of the top players in the conservative, traditional United Kingdom competed, all but one were using polyester flights—and he was using paper.

Molded plastic flights—the sort you see on toys—last longer than the others, but they are dowdy things with no class. Even so, many top players use them, including Tony Money.

Paper flights are cheap and fly true, but are not durable.

Polyester flights may last longer than feathers but when they finally split, the game is over, while feathers can get quite tatty and still do their job. When another dart splits the feather fronds, a stroke of the fingers will set things right, and a gentle steaming can partly rejuvenate all but the very worst cases.

One American player says the difference between feather and poly flights is that with feathers, "you don't throw as hard. Feathers add lift; with feathers the point might even lift up if it's thrown hard. Poly flights are for the harder throwers."

McLeod, who talks to everybody and thinks about these things, says, "With a feather you can float it in, curve it, work with it, give it English. Many players do this without realizing it. With feathers you have a more precise feel of the dart, and more directability. Polyester flights must be thrown exactly the same each time. They're perfect, so *you* have to be."

The main flights argument is over the deflection problem. Say you have thrown one dart into the triple-20 bed. Then you throw a second dart for the same place. It is a tiny spot, and the chances are quite high of the second dart hitting the first one and being knocked off course. It happens frequently, especially among good players who throw tight groupings.

Feather buffs claim that the second dart will pass undeflected through the fronds of the first dart's feather flights, flying on to the mark. The hard poly flights might knock it aside.

But the poly proponents claim an equal benefit: If the poly flight of the second dart hits the first dart, that flight will pop harmlessly out, leaving the barrel and point to finish the last inch or two of the trip undeflected.

This becomes much clearer when you have actually seen it happen a few times. The main thing is this: The feather buffs and the poly proponents are really talking about two different situations—though they occur with about equal frequency—and both of them have a point.

One manufacturer, Kwiz, has tried to solve the deflection problem with a flight called the Springbak, feathers connected to the shaft with a spiral spring which allows them to flex laterally under pressure. For some players, they may work well.

So the choice of darts and flights comes down again to experimentation, to empirical testing, to feel and compatibility. And a good bit of it is psychological. Many good players throw as well with one dart as with another, but if they doubt their equipment they find it as hard to concentrate as if they had to go to the bathroom—a condition in which all players agree (they call it

Rule 53) that it is folly to try to aim a dart. In a game of such delicate balances, these things all make a difference. They truly do.

DARTBOARDS

Olly Croft and Frosty were standing at the bar in a pub called The Spurs, drinking lager and arguing genially about dartboards.

"No door," Frosty seemed to be saying.

"Win more," replied Olly.

There are two major brands of serious dartboards, Nodor and Winmau, and Olly and Frosty were pronouncing them correctly. Olly would reel off a series of putative Winmau virtues, and Frosty would reply with a series he attributed to Nodor.

"Consistency of wires."

"Longer lasting."

"Won't deteriorate in a hot climate."

"Colors won't run."

Back in the U.S.A. Conrad Daniels pondered the question for a very short time and said: "There is no important difference between them."

Many players have a preference, but for most people Daniels is probably right. The two manufacturers split the bristle board market about evenly.

If you asked a dart player what material goes into the top-quality "bristle board" he plays on every night, three-to-one he would answer hog bristles, and be quite mistaken. Both Nodor and Winmau are made of compressed tufts of sisal, a vegetable fiber commonly used in rope and doormats. Since it was invented in the early 1930s—after a player noticed how neatly his bounced-out dart stuck into a doormat, or so the story goes—the bristle board has overtaken the classic elm board to the point where the elm board is, like American darts, a dying institution.

The elm board is still a beautiful thing, however, with a great aura of tradition surrounding it, and there are few sounds in the world so evocative as the gentle *tok* of a dart landing in real wood. The elm board is made of laminated elmwood two inches thick, scribed for numbers, dyed with color, and affixed with the usual metal "spider."

Handsome as it is, the elm board is an enormous pain in the neck. Because it is wood, the board would crack if left to dry, so it must be soaked overnight every day or so, gulping in nearly six pints of water. Wood floats, so manufacturers have devised special soaking tubs that keep them fully immersed, though in most pubs where they are used the landlord simply drops them into a wide basin and piles a few bricks on top. Many publicans have two elm boards, one to play on, and one to soak. But life is too short for this sort of thing, and the soaking can rust the wire spider, or turn the board's face slimy, or make it smell. At tournaments, they are all but impossible. "There is no way to get sixteen of them together, all wet at the same time," says Olly Croft. "And the color runs."

For most serious play, then, the bristle boards are best. Who had the original idea is subject to conflicting claims, but one of the firms has a curious history. It began as the No Odour Modelling Company of Stratford, founded by a London schoolmaster and industrial chemist named Leggatt. Leggatt had invented a substitute for the old-fashioned kind of smelly modeling clay used by schoolchildren, just as good but *sans* reek. He cast about for other ways of marketing the stuff and somehow thought of making dartboards. He fabricated a few and sold them. They failed to catch on, although some are still seen in the Midlands where they are used with wooden French darts. The problem with clay dartboards was that they had to be rolled smooth again at the conclusion of every match, which made them even more trouble than elm boards. But Leggatt apparently liked the idea of making dartboards; he began using sisal, and before long had retired to the West Indies.

All bristle boards are made similarly. Machines compress long skeins of sisal into a continuous "pipe" some three inches in diameter and wrap them in brown paper. Other machines chop off inch-thick "biscuits" of the material, and about fifty of these —weighing six and a quarter pounds—are allotted to each board. They are given a fiberboard backing, then put into a press and mashed into a dartboard. The surface is sanded, the board immersed in fungicide, and then sprayed with the color pattern and hand-wired with a galvanized spider that will withstand, so they say, a dart traveling at forty miles an hour.

A Nodor innovation has been thin steel bands sunk into the board's surface, instead of wires on the surface, to delineate the segments. Though the steel bands can only be used on the circular portions (radials are still hand-wired) they are thinner and provide more scoring area and reduce bounce-out, or so Nodor claims. So far as I can learn, however, these are not yet available in America.

The standard clock-face board—also called the London, English, trebles, or Number One board—is the one used in nearly all official competitions, but it is not the only board made. There is of course the American dartboard described in Chapter Three. In England, a dozen other boards have sprung up over the years, along with different games to be played on them. They, like American darts, appear to be dying out, but are worth mentioning not only for their historical interest but because some of the finest players in the world learned to play on them. Nodor still makes seven different kinds for the English market, although 80 percent of the firm's production is of the clock-face board, and it is the only one they export.

Of the unusual boards, the two most popular are the Yorkshire, which is much like the clock-face board but with a smaller bull and no triples ring (it is still widely used in Northern England), and the Northern Irish board—all black, with a small single bull and no triples ring. These two are still in production, but demand for the others is so slight, says Nodor, that they are virtually made to order. There is the Burton or Staffordshire board, with a small single bull, no triples ring, and two tiny diamond shapes outside the island (between 4-13 and between 9-4) as additional scoring areas worth twenty-five points each; the Lincoln board, which looks like the black Irish board except that its playing area is only fifteen inches in diameter, and two different "Fives" boards. The "Wide Fives," "London Fives," or "Ipswich" board has half as many segments as usual, but they are double-wide, and numbered only with five, ten, fifteen, and twenty, with a double bull and both a triples and a doubles ring. The "Narrow Fives" or "Competition Fives" board is similar, except the doubles and triples rings are thinner. There is also a Manchester, or "log-end" board, black, made of elm, with a ten-inch playing area, no triples ring, and a very narrow doubles ring. There was once a Tonbridge board, with a triples ring at the very outside and a diamond shape inside that counted double, and there was a Club board which had a small bull in each segment instead of a triples ring.

The thrust toward standardization has driven most of these boards into small local niches in Britain, where they survive as oddities. Their doom appears sealed.

New players have the option of starting out with a spun-paper dartboard, which is cheap but not durable, or a cork dartboard, which has become rare because it also wears out rapidly, or a bristle board. In the United States bristle boards cost $30–$35, last indefinitely, and need no maintenance beyond occasionally turning the movable spider so that different segments serve as the heavily used 20s and wear evenly.

For the record, here are some dimensions.

The actual playing area, measured across the board from one outer doubles wire to the other, is 13¼ inches in diameter.

From the center of the bull to the outer triples wire is 4⅛ inches.

Any given double is 2 inches by ⅜ inches.

Any given triple is 1⅛ inches by ⅜ inches.

Diameter of the entire bull is 1¼ inches.

Diameter of the (red) double bull is ½ inch.

Optimists mount their dartboards directly on the wall. But even the best shooter can miss the board entirely when going for a double, so it seems best to protect any surrounding areas the owner cares about. One way is to buy a dartboard cabinet, a number of which are available, most with doors that open to reveal the board and a scoreboard, some with lights. Another, cheaper, way is to fabricate a plywood backboard—size depending on the skill of players expected to compete; plywood comes as large as four-by-ten feet—finishing it as your personal aesthetic dictates. Some players cover them with carpet. Other players use a halved auto tire to encircle the dartboard, and a few like to embellish these with white paint, which one dartist thinks is an error. White reflects light, he says, causing the pupils to dilate and impeding vision.

A dartboard does need good illumination, preferably a light of its own. Some use a big spotlight above the board (although

McLeod believes the heat from these can create an "air pocket" that deflects the dart). Others use a small but powerful tensor-type lamp. I have one of these, but find that it does not illuminate the board evenly, and throws shadows. The best method I have seen uses long white fluorescent tubes above the board: they are cool, throw less shadow, and use less electricity.

SCOREBOARDS

These abound, and among the best is still the traditional blackboard. They come plain and fancy, the fancy ones with a painted grid for scoring American cricket games, and lines that show you where to write the numbers in 301. There are also lucite boards—costing about $20—designed for use with grease pencils.

The most imaginative are the futuristic electronic scoreboards, some of which, I am told, sell for as much as $8,000—if true, this is a cheerful rip-off I have been unable to track down.

Five young English engineering students spent thirteen weeks developing a dartboard embedded with sensors and a computer-controlled display panel that shows a running total of each player's score without anyone ever having to lift a piece of chalk. When darts are removed from the board the computer switches off, and the system is reactivated when the next player steps onto the special throwing mat in which a concealed "proximity indicator" lurks, and a light goes on to show the system is prepared for the throw. This cunning device can be programmed for 301, 501, or 1,001, and you can tell it whether or not an opening double is required. There is even a light that comes on when a player busts. They call this item Arachnid, which of course is the generic name for spider, which of course is the metaphoric name for the metal web on the dartboard.

Question: If this tiresome trend continues, will some canny fellow develop an electronic scoreboard for pubs, so that you have to feed it a quarter in order to play a game and get your score?

Of course. As a matter of fact, one is already working on it. The less said about this the better.

I know a man who is a fanatical camera buff. He owns a Nikon with full range of lenses, filters, and cases. He has a Hasselblad with ditto. He has a collection of little spy-type cameras, and a fully outfitted darkroom. He subscribes to all the magazines, buys all the books from Steichen to Flip Schulke to Jill Freedman to Duane Michals, from Mathew Brady to Diane Arbus. He enrolls in advanced creative photography courses at the local university, talks about photographic equipment with a zealot's enthusiasm, and can take a single glance at a photograph by any of two hundred important photographers of the last hundred years and tell you which one made it. I have hardly known him to take a picture.

There are hi-fi nuts like him, with a houseful of components and no records, no discernible love of music—it's the gear they love.

What with all the dart gear on the market and the vast range of darts you can assemble with it, the same trap is tempting. Of course it is good clean fun to those it interests, but the only important thing about darting equipment is that it is just not all that important. Joe Hitchcock says a great darts player is born, not made, that it is a gift, not a reward, and he throws well enough with nails to suggest there is truth in what he says. Roger Messer grins: "One of the best players I know plays with a set of old brass barrels, a stick cut from the hedgerow, and a bus ticket for a flight."

Though most top players pay a certain amount of attention to what the English call kit, and some switch equipment from time to time, they seem to do so as much for the psychic boost of a fresh start, a rebirth, as for any substantive gains the gear might offer. And an hour's worth of practice is probably worth more than a dollar's worth of new darts.

TUFF DARTS

Ed McDevitt, a fine American player from Philadelphia, was at a tournament once clutching a fistful of ill-assorted darts. He had aluminum shafts on one, nylon on another, plastic flights here and feather flights there, and indeed he must have looked comical. But when somebody laughed, McDevitt said it all.

"It ain't the brush that paints the picture, pal, it's the artist."

 6

MUGGS AWAY
FORTY GAMES
AND HOW TO PLAY THEM

Stopping in at a Manhattan darts pub one evening I found Greg Walsh, a tall, thin carpet salesman, standing beside the bar with a beer in one hand and his darts in the other. He was waiting for his challenge to come up, so we chatted about various games you can play with darts. "Have you ever played this one?" he said after a few minutes, and reached into his hip pocket.

Walsh's turn had come, and he took a dollar bill from his

wallet and borrowed two darts from a friend. Then he walked to the dartboard and pinned the dollar bill horizontally across the center of it so that the bull's-eye was obscured.

"Okay," he said, "You get three shots. One from two feet, one from the standard eight feet, and one from ten feet."

I stared at the dollar, which seemed reasonably sizable. "What do I have to hit? The numbers in the corners? What's-his name's face there in the middle?"

"Just hit the dollar is all," Walsh said and delivered what can only be described as a smirk.

"From two feet? You're kidding."

"Two, eight, and ten." He smirked some more.

From two feet the dollar bill looked like Texas. I could have reached out and stuck the dart into it without letting go. I glanced at Walsh, turned back to face the dollar, and threw the dart.

It stuck in the board two inches above the dollar bill.

Walsh was not the only one who laughed.

From eight feet the dollar bill looked like a dollar bill. I missed Washington's nose but hit the bill, just a little off center.

Somebody said drily, "Good dart."

From ten feet the dollar bill looked as far away as a very small village in Rhode Island, and it turned out to be as hard to hit from the West Side of Manhattan. I missed an inch low.

"It's a lot harder than it looks," Walsh said. "Sometimes you put a dollar in the pot and pitch in a dollar for every miss. Best shooter gets the pot. It's a good change-of-pace game."

He smirked again and went away to take down his dollar bill with the single hole in it. It was still spendable.

It must be possible to play darts for days on end without playing the same game twice; there are an infinite number of variations possible on the few major themes, plus variations of rule and custom that differ from place to place—length of throw, whether or not slops, or fallout, counts in games like Cricket, whether or not it is permissible to attempt a one-dart, triple-out-shot in a —01 game. And sooner or later most players will get temporarily bored with standard games, or will perceive a new way the board can be arranged in one's mind to create a new game, and invent one. The various dart games are merely a framework within which to experience the central challenge, anyway, which is to hit a fly-sized spot every time, at will, from eight feet away with a needle-sized point, the fly-sized spot hopping from place to place all over the board from throw to throw.

Some games give the novice more slack than others, and some can only be played satisfactorily by an expert shooter. Every player knows this, but it is hard to find agreement on which games are which, and a graduate student in computer sciences could have some fun—and probably write an interesting thesis— by finding out.

Take American cricket and English 301 for example. Probably everyone who plays darts in the United States knows them both; they are played more frequently than any other games. Both are simple and clean, easily understood in their basics but difficult to play well, full of labyrinthine strategy and subsurface tension. As a dim arithmetician I enjoy Cricket because it involves less mental number-work and I can concentrate better on the throw itself. On the other hand, playing 301 is a little like beginning photography—you have to keep in mind and master the numbers that constantly shift and realign both themselves and their relative values, while at the same time composing the shot with the eye and hand.

In Bob McLeod's dart shop one day I played Bob Theide, then ranked fifth in the world, a game of 301. It was a rout, a white-wash; I never hit the first double, was never even in the game. He finished in about twelve darts. Then we played Cricket, and although he won decisively at one point I was only a single dart behind him. Theide is at least eighteen times a better player than I, of course, but something in the game of Cricket gave me a break.

Nicky Virachkul says that is his impression too. "Those who are not so good at math would rather play Cricket. You don't have to count and you also have more time to plan strategy. In 301 you just try to score like a bastard, and you have to subtract and plan ahead." As we'll see, there is more to subtracting, darts-style, than mere subtraction.

Conrad Daniels won't even talk about Cricket. He won't even play it either; one gets the impression it is too easy and sloppy for his taste. He would rather distinguish between the various forms of —01 games: "There's a considerable amount of luck in 301, and it usually gives the amateur the best shot against the top player. But the more you increase the number of points you're playing to, say to 501, the better player has a better opportunity. As a top player I'd rather play 501. It favors the top player." This is why Joe Hitchcock preferred those 25,001-point marathons.

Forty games are described in this chapter. Among them any player from raw beginner to *News of the World* champion should find a few that are just right for his level of accomplishment— probably more than a few. Cricket and 301 are listed first. After them, games are described roughly in ascending order of difficulty (*very* roughly, as nobody really knows with any precision), from those a beginner can play well enough for pleasure, through more challenging games for the average and high-average player, to master games a novice might require a week to finish.

A distinction, to begin with. There are games, which have rules. And there is The Game (or The Sport) of Darts which, whatever the game played, has customs, traditions, various regional practices. The rules are straightforward instructions in how a game is played, how it is scored, what feats a player must accomplish in order to win. The customs are unwritten and traditional, like the English constitution, and have to do with courtesy, sportsmanship, and the like. (There is also strategy, which comes later.)

Customs first. These may vary from place to place but for the most part they are obvious and generally accepted.

Dart players don't often play strangers. They introduce themselves first.

Dart players never use another's darts without permission. One night, shortly after I had started playing darts, I was dagger-stared for an hour by a player whose darts I had borrowed and then, taking them for house darts, passed along to the next two players. Finally their owner came up and muttered, "Never let anyone touch another man's darts."

Dart players sing out their score before removing their darts, and allow time for it to be verified.

Dart players retrieve their own darts after each throw, and never retrieve anyone else's except occasionally after middle for diddle.

Dart players don't talk to their opponent when he is shooting, or with anyone else, or shuffle their feet, or clatter their darts together, or drop them, or step on them and break them to create a scene as one player confessed doing, in desperation, to rattle his winning opponent in a tournament (he felt so badly about having done it that he lost).

Players don't stand and stare into the shooter's face (nor do spectators), or lean out to see where his darts have gone until he has finished shooting.

In most places, the challenger next in line to play keeps score for those playing. In some places, taking up the chalk to keep score constitutes a challenge to the winner of the present game. Winners are obliged by courtesy to accept any challenge unless they are retiring from the game. If there is a scorer, he calls out each score earned as he writes it down, and around 170 or 180 in −01 games, he begins notifying each shooter what total score he has *left*—but never what double he needs. The shooter has to figure that out for himself or herself. Scorers may touch only chalk, never darts (unless a player is physically incapable of retrieving his own darts and both players agree that the scorer will do it for him).

In most areas the winner, or winning team, continues to hold the board until beaten by a challenger or until voluntarily retiring from play. Retired winners must earn their way back into the game in the usual way, by placing their initials on the challenge list and waiting their turn.

After a loss, most players retire from the hockey with thanks for the game. If that cannot be managed, a gracious silence is best.

There is no single definitive set of rules and specifications for the game of darts; in that sense it is still in its infancy. These are the most commonly accepted, but do not be surprised if told they do not apply.

The board is 18 inches (46 centimeters) in diameter. It is hung 5 feet, 8 inches (1.72 meters) from the floor to the center of the double bull. The hockey is (usually) 8 feet (2.44 meters) from the face of the board. The thrower's toe must not cross the front edge of the hockey—this is called getting one's feet wet—although he may lean as far forward as he chooses.

Segments of the board are called segments, wedges, or innings.

The doubles ring—the narrow, outer ring—counts two times the number of the wedge it is part of.

The triples ring—the thin ring halfway into the board—counts three times the number of the wedge.

The green ring of the bull's-eye counts 25 points.

The red center bull counts 50 points, and may be used as double 25 in the —01 games.

Darts may be as small as the player likes, but no longer than 7 inches, and no heavier than 55 grams. A gram is about 1/28th of an ounce. In England the average dart used weighs around

26-28 grams. American players seem to use somewhat lighter darts.

A "throw" is three darts. A single dart, conveniently enough, is called a "dart."

All thrown darts count. Darts cannot be thrown over again, and only those sticking in the face of the board when a player retrieves them earn score. Thus, a dart that falls out before the player finishes his throw and retrieves it, or a dart that bounces off a wire and falls to the floor, or even a dart that sticks into the tail of another, earlier dart (which is called Robin Hooding and which happens with surprising frequency) does not count. There is a rare regional variation on this rule. In some areas a dart that bounces off the board may be caught in mid-air by the player and thrown again. The feat takes quick reflexes, and is not quite safe—which occasions a digression.

A standard first-aid procedure for puncture wounds is as follows:

Move the patient as little as possible. If it can be done easily, withdraw the dart so as to prevent further tissue damage when the patient is moved. In the case of a small wound, spread the edges of the puncture a bit to promote bleeding and flush debris. Make a mental note of the angle and depth of the wound and tell the doctor. Use something clean—a handkerchief, necktie, Scotch tape, team jacket, league patch—to plug the opening and stem bleeding. Take the patient to a doctor for a tetanus shot. Return to the game.

The wire divider on the dartboard—called the spider—determines close calls.

The usual way of deciding what game to play and who shoots first is called "middle for diddle." Each player throws a single dart at the bull's-eye, and the closest to the bull chooses the game and whether he will shoot first or last. A toss of a coin is also common.

If a number of players want to divide into teams, they may draw straws or, more in keeping with the traditions of the game, "splash." To splash, each player throws for the bull with his non-playing hand. The player nearest the bull is paired with the one farthest away, the next-nearest with the next-farthest, and so on.

In team play, in most games, one individual from a team shoots, then one from the other, alternately. A few games specify otherwise.

301 (AND 201, 501, 1001; 5001, 25,001, 1,000,001)

The object of the game is to reduce the score you started with to exactly zero by subtracting points from the total, and do it ahead of your opponent. But you must start on a double and no points are scored until you have "doubled-in" by hitting that initial double. Any double will do, including the red double bull. You must also finish on a double—a double that reduces your score to exactly zero. This means that if a player is close to doubling-out but has an odd number remaining as his score, he must even up his score before he can attempt the final double.

Here is the essential pattern of the game: You throw for the doubles ring or the double bull until you hit it. Now you have doubled-in, and you may begin to score points. You throw for the highest possible score, trying to rack up points. When you have reduced your score to an even number small enough for you to score precisely that number with one dart in a doubles ring—say 32 points, or double 16—you throw at that double to go out. If you do it first, you win.

Of course, life isn't that simple. If in trying to score the final double a player shoots more than the number required, he is said to have busted, or gone bust. He is not out of the game but he stops throwing until his next turn and his score is not recorded. For example, you have 3 points left. You throw a 1, evening up your score at 2. That's fine—you need a double 1 to go out. But in trying for it you hit a 20. That is too many points, and even though you have a third dart in your hand you must stop throwing. Your score reverts to 3, and it is your opponent's turn.

It is also a bust if the player ends up after a shot with only one point left. The shot does not count and his score reverts.

In league and tournament play it is usual to play best two legs out of three (score would be either 2-0, or 2-1). In busy pubs only a single game is played.

Individual players usually play 201 or 301, or occasionally 501. Teams of two usually play 501. Teams of four, six, and eight to a side often play 1,001 or more.

In some tournaments, including the *News of the World* championships, the game is 501 with no initial double required. Purists are appalled by this oversimplification of the game, but it does speed things along to hold audience attention and spare them the shock of realizing even the world's finest players sometimes have a hell of a time doubling-in. The double-out shot is always required.

In some pubs, when a player finds himself with a triple number score such as 111, 222, 333, 444, or the like, he may elect to throw one dart only at the triple of that number—perhaps the triple 2 if he has 222 points left. If he hits that triple, he wins. If he misses, the shot does not count and his throw is over. The shot must be declared in advance, and the player gets only one dart.

Until their score has fallen below 100 or so, most gifted players will attack the triple 20 as the highest scoring bed on the board. As one player says, "You live by the triple 20, you die by the triple 20." But a miss there, even a very near miss, carries penalties— to the right a single point, to the left only 5. So the less talented may choose to throw at the triple 19 with its higher flanking numbers. And a banker friend of mine whose mind works well with numbers figured out independently what others already knew: that the area of the 16 on the left side of the board permits consistently fairly high scores with less risk.

This game is obviously a game of numbers as well as throwing skill, so here are some numbers to be aware of.

The lowest number of darts in which it is possible to achieve standard scores:

201: four

301: six

501: nine

1,001: seventeen

It is commonly said that perfect games of 201 and 301 have been accomplished often, perfect 501 games occasionally. At least one record book states that the 17-dart 1,001 has never been done—but Joe Hitchcock assured me he once did it. If so, it would have required 15 triple 20s, a triple 17, and a double bull. Kim Brown of England is on record as having shot a 20-dart game of 1,001 at an exhibition, and so is Alan Glazier, also of England, who did it by hitting 100, 140, 180, 140, 180, 180 and 81 to go out on two darts.

The highest score on which one can go out with three darts is 170—two triple 20s and a double bull.

The lowest odd number that cannot be scored with three darts and end with a double is 159.

The lowest even number that cannot be scored with three darts and end with a double is 162.

The highest score attainable with three darts is 180—three triple 20s.

AMERICAN CRICKET

In 301, as in golf, you are playing essentially against yourself. Cricket is different. Like tennis, American cricket brings you face to face with an opponent and gives you a chance to prevent him from surging too far ahead. And he has the same opportunity, which means you must pay attention.

What you must do in cricket is close the numbers between 15 and 20, plus bull's-eye, by hitting each of them three times, and in addition try to score points by hitting numbers you have closed but which have not yet been closed by your opponent. The winner is the first player who closes all his numbers and *also* has more points than his opponent. When a player has closed his numbers but is behind on points, he must catch up by hitting numbers not yet closed by his opponent. Players throw for the numbers in rotation from 20 down through 15, then bull, although a player may throw for a number out of its usual order if he calls it first—which is often done for tactical reasons. Uncalled numbers hit out of turn do not count.

Here is the way it works:

Jill throws first, for the 20s as required. She hits a 20, a 5, and a 15. The 20 counts, so she has only two 20s left to close that number. But the 5 is meaningless in cricket, and she hit the 15 out of its order so that does not count either.

Then Ned throws. He gets lucky and hits a triple 20 with his first dart. His 20s are closed. He now has the option of throwing further 20s, thus earning 20 points each time he hits it (he can do this as long as Jill's 20s are not closed), or he can move on to the next number, 19, and try to close this. Say he throws another 20, and then an accidental bull. He gets 20 points. But the bull, thrown out of its proper order, does not count.

Jill is on the defensive now, but she has options. She can throw for the 20, trying to close it to prevent Ned from earning more points there. Or, she can call another number that Ned has not closed, say the 19, and try to close it before he does and then score points on it to catch up and pass him (but she will have to go back later and close the 20s). She opts to do this. She is playing extraordinarily well. She hits a double 19 on her first dart, then a single 19 on her second. She has closed the 19s. She throws her third dart and is again lucky, hitting another double 19. She has earned 38 points and is now ahead.

They play on in this fashion until, nearing the end, Ned has 60 points and a single bull left to have all his numbers closed. Jill has closed all the numbers, but has only 38 points.

If Jill is to win she must pass Ned in points before he closes his final bull, and the only way she can get points is to throw into an area Ned has not closed. The only one left is the bull. If she hits the bull, thus earning either 25 or 50 points, she wins, since she is both closed and ahead on points. If she misses, it becomes Ned's turn. If he hits and closes the bull he needs, then since he is ahead on points and now closed, he wins.

In this example, both Jill and Ned have thrown fine darts; for the average player things won't always go quite this smoothly. Also, this is the sternest version of cricket, in which "slops" or "fallout" do not count. In a gentler version that is good for beginning players, darts may be thrown at any of the numbers between 15 and 20, and bull, in any order, so that accidental hits, say into the 16 when actually aiming for the 19, will be counted.

HIGH SCORE

A fast game any number can play. Rules are simple. Players designate a number to play for, often 1,000 points. The first player to reach or surpass this number wins.

SCRAM

This is an excellent game, played in two parts. In the first half, one player is Scorer, the other is Stopper.

The Scorer writes a list of the numbers 1 to 20, plus bull, plus double bull if desired. The Stopper shoots first. He tries to hit any number, and every time he hits one it is closed, no longer active, and the Scorer crosses it off his list.

After each turn by the Stopper, the Scorer throws. His job is to hit any number not already killed by the Stopper. For each hit he scores points in the usual way. Thus, his choice of targets narrows as the first half of the game progresses and the Stopper closes numbers.

When the Stopper has narrowed the Scorer's possibilities to zero by closing all the numbers and bulls, the half is over. The Scorer adds up his point total if he hasn't been keeping a running tally. The players switch roles and play again. Highest score wins.

This is an elementary but amusingly cutthroat game.

SUDDEN DEATH

An elimination game for eight or more. Each player shoots for the highest possible score. After each throw, the player scoring lowest drops out until one player, the winner, remains. When two or more players tie for lowest score on a given throw, both or all drop out.

ROUND THE CLOCK

Among other things this is a good practice game that can be played alone or in groups. Five variations are given here, from simple to fairly challenging.

Basic Round the Clock

Any number can play. Scoring can be done in your head. The idea is to go round the board placing one dart any place in each wedge in sequence, 1 through 20. The first to reach and hit the 20 wins. Or you can require a bullshot at the end—1 through 20, plus bull. A perfect game would be to accomplish this in 20 darts, or 21 if bull were added.

Round the Clock 2

Same as above, only each player must hit a double (any double) before starting on the 1 to 20 sequence. He must also finish by scoring one in the bull and one in the triple 20. A perfect game would be 23 darts.

Round the Clock 3

More difficult. You must start on a double 1, hit each section 2 through 19, and finish with a double 20, a bull, and a triple 20. A perfect game: 22 darts.

Round the Clock 4

More difficult still. Object is to go round the clock in *doubles*, starting on double 1, hitting each double in sequence through double 20, then a bull and triple 20. A perfect game is 22 darts.

Round the Clock 5

Very difficult. Starting on any double, go around the clock to 19 in *triples*, finish with a double 20 and then three double bulls. In this game, whenever a player scores with all three darts of a throw, he gets a free throw. A perfect game would be to accomplish all this in 24 darts.

SHOVE-HA'PENNY

This is darts metaphor for another English pub game. Only the numbers 1 through 9 are used. Singles are worth one point, doubles two, triples three. Each player may throw at any of the nine numbers he chooses when his turn comes up. The object is to score three in each of the nine designated wedges before the other players do so. A player who scores more than three points in any one number must give the excess to the player folowing, or in another version, to the player most in need of points in that wedge. But the winning shot must be scored by the winner, not handed to him by an opponent. Theoretically the game can be won in three throws—nine darts in nine triples.

SHANGHAI

This is both a game and a concept.

The concept first. If local rules permit, any appropriate game can be won by a player calling and then throwing a Shanghai. A Shanghai is accomplished with three darts of the same throw, one entering the single, one the double, and one the triple of the same wedge. It *must* be called in advance. If the player is successful in Shanghai-ing, he automatically wins. In many regions, however, the final dart of a Shanghai must be either a double or a triple. In some places, a player can call his intention to Shanghai after placing one or two of the darts. If a Shanghai attempt fails, the player scores no points for that throw.

The game. Shanghai is similar to Round the Clock and is also for any number of players. At each wedge from 1 to 20 the player is limited to three darts. The idea is to score as many points in each wedge as possible. Highest score at the end of 20 wedges wins. Maximum possible score: 1,890. Naturally, a Shanghai thrown at any point wins the game. This is the only game in which the intention to Shanghai need not be called beforehand.

SHANGHAI 2

Any number can play. Players throw three darts at each number from 1 to 7, trying for the highest possible numerical score. After seven throws the highest score wins.

However: Before the game begins some particular number is designated the Shang. Often this is the 3. Any player who misses this number with all three darts of a throw must see his score reduced to zero.

However again: The 5 is called the Hai. Any player who misses the 5 with all three darts must drop out of the game.

However once more: There is also the usual Shanghai, and any player who accomplishes it wins the game on the spot, regardless of the score.

SHANGHAI 3

Winner of middle for diddle chooses not only which six numbers will be played, but where in the playing order he will throw. Players throw for the six predesignated numbers in order, then for the doubles ring (any double) and the triples ring (any triple), then the bull. Whenever a given player fails to hit the number or ring in play with a given throw, his score is halved. Play continues until one player scores a Shanghai in the traditional manner. Then the Shanghai-ing player adds his Shanghai point total to his previous point total, then takes 100 points each from the scores of all the other players and adds *them* to his point total. And then he figures the difference between his score and the other players' various scores, and adds all those figures to his own score. If another player still has more points at this stage of the game, the Shanghai-ing player receives another 100-point bonus.

After all of this the Shanghai-ing player is expected to win, and perhaps he does. I enjoy darts too much to play such a game.

HALVE IT

This is an English game similar to Shanghai 3. Begin by designating certain numbers, say 10, 16, 20, and 50 (the double bull). Players throw for them in turn from lowest to highest number, aiming three darts at each. Any player who misses his first number with all three darts of the throw begins the game *minus* whatever his score would have been had he struck it with one dart—minus 10, for instance, had 10 been the first number. This is deducted from any subsequent score he earns. Whenever a player fails to hit his required number within the three allowed darts, moreover, he halves his score. If for instance Barbara had 40 points, and throws for the 16 three times and misses all three, her point total will be halved to 20. Play continues until a player reaches some predetermined score, often 201.

WARFARE

One player or team is entrenched in the top half of the board, numbers 11 through 13, and the other is dug in on the lower, numbers 6 through 8. The objective is to defeat the enemy by killing off his soldiers, each expendable footslogging grunt being represented by some given portion of the board. To make the game easy, you could simply designate each wedge as a soldier. To make it more challenging, you could designate Soldier Number One as the triple 3, Soldier Number Two as the upper half of the single bull, and so on, writing these down on the scoreboard beforehand and keeping a body count as the casualties pile up. If you do the latter, make certain the two armies are evenly equipped—with an equal number of hard and easy shots on both sides. Players or teams throw alternately as the slaughter begins, and the victor is the side that first accomplishes a massacre. Within the rules, of course.

CASTLE

This is an English game related as follows by Keith Naylor in *Darts World* magazine:

"Each player throws a dart with the wrong hand and the number scored is to be his castle. With the treble counting three, double two and single one the object is for each player to score 15 of his own number to complete the castle. (A picture of a castle can actually be drawn on the board in 15 lines.) A player can either throw to build his own castle up or he can throw at his opponent's number in order to knock down his castle."

Unfortunately, Mr. Naylor does not explain how to draw a castle.

KNOCKOUT

A game for two or more players. Each throws with his opposite hand for the number that will become "his" double. Then each player throws in turn for any double but his own, trying to knock others out of the game by hitting their double three times. When a player's double has been hit three times by the others, it is killed and he is knocked out of the game. Last player in the game wins. This is good practice for doubling-in and doubling-out in 301.

KILLER

A very good game if you have a large number of players. The object is to "kill" the other players before being set upon and slain oneself. Final survivor wins.

To begin, each player throws a dart with his opposite hand, or underhand, to establish "his" or "her" number. More than one player may own the same number.

Players throw in turn and try, by hitting the double of any opponent's number, to eliminate that opponent. Every dart in a player's double counts as one, and when a player's double is hit five times (by one or any combination of his opponents) he is killed and should lie down. (The morbid imagery in these games is probably inevitable.) If more than one player have that number, all are dead.

It is ethical in Killer, if not entirely nice, to gang up on better players and mug them. Those sharing a number and whose interests therefore coincide may also team up against the others. If teams like this develop and one of them wins, the only way to establish a single final winner is to play off. Members of the winning team throw for new numbers. Each of the players then assumes the number of hits that had been scored against their common number during the previous game, and the new game proceeds as before.

For instance, three players in the first game own the same number. Playing cooperatively, they win, although three hits were scored against their number before they managed to kill off the opposition. They will play off. They rethrow for new numbers. Two of them again hit the same number. The two, as a team, now assume three points against them and the odd man does the same. If the team scores the remaining necessary two points against the odd man, driving him out, they must rethrow once more and play off between themselves. If the individual beats the team, he is the winner. It is not as complicated as it sounds.

BLIND KILLER

For five or more players, a merrier sort of game than you'd guess from its handle. It is the same as Killer except that the numbers 1 through 20 are written on slips of paper, placed in a hat (only a hat will do), and a number drawn by each player. Players do not divulge their numbers. This will be the player's double; as in Killer, others begin throwing for various doubles except that nobody knows which double is whose, if anybody's, leading to much anxiety and many nervous witticisms. Any player who loses a third life must say so and drop out. Last one alive wins.

GOLF

As in real golf the player achieving the lowest score wins. Wedges are referred to as holes and the game is scored as follows: each double scores 1, each triple scores 2, the wedge between triple and bull scores 3, and the wedge between double and triple scores 4. A miss scores 5. The game is played to 18 holes.

Hazards exist, however. Only the player's *last* dart thrown at a given hole counts for score. And a player may choose to stop playing any hole at any time, making the dart just thrown his last.

Here's an example. Arnie throws one dart, hits the area between the bull and the triple which gives him 3 points, and declares, "That's my last dart." He stops throwing. Johnny, his opponent, then throws a dart into the same area, giving himself 3 points and a dilemma. Johnny can decide to stop throwing right then, keeping his 3 points and a tie for the hole. Or he may decide to throw again, trying for a lower score in either the double or triple ring. Say he does this and his dart lands in the area between the double and the triple rings, which is worth 4 points. He has failed to get lower than Arnie on the hole; in fact he has worsened his position. Still, he has a third dart. He elects to throw it. The dart goes outside the playing area—"off the island"

and into the rough, to mix a few metaphors—and Johnny is stuck with 5 points for the hole. Maximum score per hole is 5, minimum is 1. Par is 54.

FOLLOW THE LEADER

For any number of players. Middle for diddle for first throw. The idea is to become a tough act to follow. The first player throws three darts anywhere he or she chooses, attempting to accomplish a difficult shot especially with the last one. The next player must place *one* of his or her three darts in the same portion of the board as the final dart of the previous player, or lose one life. Three lives lost equals death, or anyway early retirement from the game which amounts to the same thing. When a player is forced out, the next player must throw for whatever section of the board the last dart of the retired player fell into. Triples, doubles, large singles, small singles, bull, and double bull are each separate segments. Survivor wins.

NINE LIVES

A variation on the Round the Clock theme, a game of elimination for any number. Each player begins the game with three lives (not nine; I can't explain this, it's just another tradition). In sequence, players try to throw a dart each into innings 1 through 20. Each player has three darts to hit each inning. Whenever he misses an inning with three darts, he loses a life. Losing three, he dies. Unused darts from one throw can be carried over into the next inning—if Morris hits number 1 on his first dart he can try for number 2 with his remaining two darts, and if he hits 2 on the second dart he can try for number 3.

Nine Lives, a variation

Keep score for each inning, doubles and triples counting as 2 and 3 points. The player scoring lowest in each inning loses a life.

FORTY GAMES AND HOW TO PLAY THEM

RALLY

A game for any number based pretty loosely on auto racing. Start by laying out a rally route on the board, with obstacles and a finish line. Players can agree on any combination of wedges, doubles, triples, or bulls to represent (this requires a little imagination) hairpin curves, potholes, burning wrecks, pools of spilled oil, and rubbernecking spectators. Obstacles are created by designating certain difficult spots to hit twice or more before moving on.

A sample route: single 7, single 4, inner 12, single 2, obstacle (two triple 20s), double 6, single 14, outer 19, obstacle (double bull), single 3, and finish on two bulls and a checkered flag. Always finish on two bulls, either one double or two singles. First across the line wins.

BASEBALL

Any number can play. Use innings 1 through 9. Each player throws three darts at each inning in sequence 1 through 9. The inning being thrown at is the live inning, and only darts striking it count. Score 1 run for a dart in the single, 2 for a double, 3 for a triple. In team play members of a team throw together, then members of the other team. Tied games are played off in extra innings. Highest possible score in nine innings: 21.

BULL'S-EYE BASEBALL

Same theme as Baseball except that each player or team must hit a bull's-eye before runs can be scored in each inning. If no bull is hit—no score. Only runs batted in *after* the bull is hit count. If a player hits more than one bull while shooting for a given inning, the number of runs he scored in that inning is multiplied by the number of bulls hit. Thus, if Henry hit a double bull and then a single and a double—4 runs—he would take a score for that inning of 8.

14 STOP

Another Baseball variation most interestingly played by two-person teams. Singles may play if individuals assume both roles of the team function.

The first player of a team throws at the 14, which he must hit if his team is to participate further in the inning. If he misses the 14, no points are scored for the inning. If he hits, he has the option of stopping with that dart, or throwing any or all of his remaining darts at the 14. Each dart placed in the 14 allows the other member of the team to score in whatever baseball inning is alive at the moment, and to multiply his score by the number of 14s his partner threw.

For instance Ted and Susan are a team. Ted throws two 14s, then stops. Susan comes up to throw for the live inning, which happens to be 3. She scores 5 runs. Ted and Susan multiply her 5 runs by his two 14s, and their score for the inning becomes 10.

The complication is in the Stop. Ted's option to stop throwing 14s can be exercised at any moment except just before a miss. Had he thrown a third dart and missed the 14, there would have been no score for Susan (and him). Should Susan fail to score in the live inning it's a strikeout no matter how many 14s he delivered—no score.

CHASE OR FOXHUNT

A game for two or more teams or players. Middle for diddle to start, nearest to bull becoming fox and farthest hound. The fox starts on double 20 and must throw a double and a single in each wedge, traveling counterclockwise around the board and back to 20.

The hound chases her. He starts on the double 18, two paces behind, and pursues the fox by throwing doubles only. This gives him a chance to close the gap. The point at which he catches up is recorded and fox and hound swap roles and play again. Winner is the player who, as fox, gets farthest before being brought to ground. It takes a wily fox indeed to elude the hound altogether and dart back into its burrow in the 20 wedge.

HIGHJUMP

The object of this game is to jump high, but figuratively. The increments of altitude are measured off by designating the double 3 as lowest point, and moving up through large 3, triple 3, small 3, 25, double bull, 25, small 20, triple 20, large 20, and double 20 at the top of the board. Players throw alternately and get three tries at each height as they attempt to move from the bottom of the board to the top. If a player misses at any height, he is out and the last successful jump he has made is his height record for the game. Highest hopper wins.

This is a difficult game.

BROADJUMP

Precisely the same as Highjump except that the game is played from left to right across the board instead of from bottom to top. It is slightly easier for that reason, at least on the doubles and triples.

MIDDLE FOR DIDDLE

This is a game for two invented by Noel Williamson, who is famous in England for his charmingly cheerful verse on the subject of darts. It is included in his book *Darts*.

"Two players each throw a dart for the centre of the board to see who starts first. Nearest the bull throws for a double, and each player after obtaining a double then throws for bulls and 25s until arriving at a finishing double. Trebles and doubles outside the treble circle do not count in the scoring, but numbers inside the treble circle all count toward the player's score. The more 'bulls' and 25s scored, therefore, the sooner the game is finished. A total of 501 must be scored to win."

TIC-TAC-TOE

An active version of the sedentary pencil-and-paper game. Start by imagining a nine-box grid on the dartboard, formed by the numbers 12, 20, 18, 11, bull, 6, 7, 3, 2. Players alternate throwing *one* dart apiece, the object being to close three numbers that form a vertical, horizontal, or diagonal straight line before one's opponent does so. A bull, obviously, is always necessary. A player may close an opponent's needed number to prevent completion of the tic-tac-toe. Ties must be replayed.

Tic-Tac-Toe, a variation

Played exactly the same way except that the straight line must be composed of three doubles: two doubled numbers in a straight line plus the double bull at the center.

WICKETS OR ENGLISH CRICKET

A bit of a parallel to the British outdoor game, also known in Indian Rocks Beach, Florida, as Beavers and Otters. One player or team bats and the other bowls, and they alternate throwing. The Batsman begins the game with nine wickets, and the Bowler must capture them. The Bowler does this by throwing bull's-eyes, a single 25 earning him one wicket and a double bull earning him two. During the first half of the game all the Bowler does is throw bulls, or try to. Meanwhile, the Batsman is trying to score runs. He does this by throwing at any wedge he chooses, doubles and triples multiplying the face value.

However: Only those points over 40 in a throw are counted for the Batsman's score. If he scores 48 in a throw, for instance, he gets 8 points. If he scores 41, he gets 1. If he scores 40 or under, he gets no points.

However once again: The Batsman may not throw at the bull, even accidentally. If he hits it, he loses a wicket (or 2 if he hits the double bull).

The Bowler has a penalty to watch for too: Each time a dart of his lands outside the triple ring, that numerical score goes to the Batsman.

When the Bowler has captured his 9 wickets, the half-game is over and the players reverse roles. Highest score after two halves wins the game.

SOCCER

For two players or teams. Only doubles and bulls are in play. Middle for diddle to start and nearest to bull shoots first. His objective is to gain possession of the ball by throwing a bull's-eye. Ball in hand, he may then attempt to score a goal, which he does by hitting any double. Once he scores a bull and has the ball he continues to throw doubles—scoring goals—until the ball is taken from him by his opponent, who must do this in the same way, by hitting the bull's-eye. Players throw alternately. First to reach 10 goals is the winner. A good practice game.

FOOTBALL

A scrimmage for as many as 20 players. Start by agreeing on a number of points or time limit that will end the game.

If only two players or teams play, choose two wedges directly opposite one another. One wedge belongs to one team and the other to the other team. Alternating throws in the usual way, and picking up where play left off the throw before, the player tries to score a goal by marching down his own end of the field, past the 50-yard line (the bull), and up his opponent's end to the goal line. This takes a minimum of 11 darts and is done by hitting each division of the board in sequence including doubles, triples, and large and small singles. For fine players this game can be a real Superbowl. For ordinary ones, it is merely tiresome.

MUGGS AWAY

51 IN 5S OR ALL FIVES

Any number can play and all areas of the board are used. Each player must score a number divisible by five with each throw. Any total number scored in a throw that is indivisible by five does not yield points. Further, a player's last dart of a throw must lie in a scoring bed in order for that throw to yield points—if it falls out or misses a number needed to make a five-divisible final score, even if the two previous darts add up to a five multiple, he gets no score.

For each five points obtained in this rather arbitrary way, the player gets one point. To finish the game and go out he must hit the exact score needed to earn him 55 points. Scoring may be by subtraction from 51 or accumulation to 51, this being one of the few options you get in this game.

Hint: After a few games the player begins to see the safest scoring areas—the wide 10-15 wedge being the most noticeable.

MULLIGAN

A very demanding game for advanced players; the only thing simple about Mulligan is the rules. Players mutually agree on seven innings, either in sequence or randomly scattered. Each player must score *three* triples in each inning before going on to the next. After earning his 21 triples he must then shoot three double bulls to go out. The first to do so wins the game. Mulligan establishes the outer limits of darting challenge.

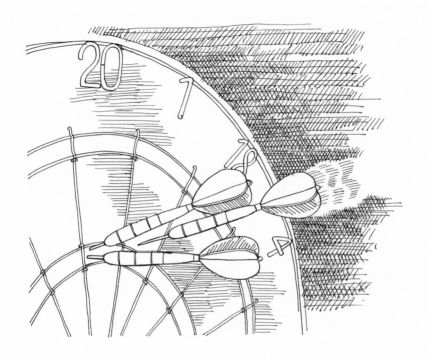

THREE IN A BED
TIPS AND STRATEGIES
FOR WINNING

At the four-hundred-year-old Queen's Head pub in Newton, Cambridgeshire, one day in 1965, the neighborhood blokes were having a jolly game of darts when the Shah of Iran stopped in with Queen Farah and the royal entourage. After observing curiously for a few minutes, the couple asked whether they might examine a set of darts—which of course they could, the English having much affection for royalty, even other people's.

The queen went over to the hockey, set herself, and nonchalantly threw three darts, scoring three bull's-eyes.

As for the shah, he threw only two. Both of them bounced off the board and he gave up.

Queen Farah shrugged, or did whatever it is that Iranian queens do when they wish to express ho-hum, and said, "The harder you try at this game, the more difficult it is."

This was perceptive of the queen, and very sharp all around. Not many people—beginners or not—can hit the bull three times in a row, and not many beginners can offer a tip that even experts might profit from.

This chapter is basic darts, a discussion of how to play not brilliantly—good players teach themselves that—but merely well. From the start it was clear that nobody—expert or novice—would profit much from knowing what the author knows about throwing a dart, but I spent a happy year talking with hundreds of players, including some of the top international ones, and in the time-honored tradition of the awed third-rater, sought advice from them all. That, mostly, is what this chapter is about.

The new player should be able to extract or distill a bit of wisdom from it all, even if only the knowledge that copying an expert down to his shoelaces and brand of beer won't necessarily make you an expert too. But you already guessed that. It's part of the code of life: To excel, start by copying the excellent. Then go your own way.

Playing a fine game of darts unifies the physical and the mental, the emotional and the mathematical. Stance, grip, and throw melt into one act; concentration and tactics are faces of the same creature, often elusive. The expert dartist throwing for his final double is a rallied organism: coiled but composed, tense but serene, graceful and delicate, yet sharp.

If learning is largely imitative, it is not always easy to know whom to imitate. Within the strict boundaries of the game, the variety of styles and theories of performance are legion. Even after you learn what to look for, observing two players is like watching Ashe and Graebner play tennis: For good or ill, the style of play follows the player's temperament. One is erratic but occasionally inspired. Another is rigid but consistent.

In darts, similarly. One will whip in his darts in rapid succession, machinelike; another will aim like a timid golfer lining up a putt. Some take so long planning each toss they are accused of plotting a psych-out; but the *News of the World* winner in 1950 threw three darts every four seconds. One player tosses with such an abbreviated stroke that his dart seems to leap from nose to board without assistance; another winds up like a baseball pitcher, mixes in an array of body English, and lets go with the energy of an Olympic hammer-thrower. One stands two feet to one side of the hockey and throws on an acute angle; another is the Statue of Liberty, his arm starting almost straight above his head, driving the dart downward. One employs a flat, sharp trajectory; another lobs. A giant of nearly seven feet throws side-arm. In East Anglia, players throw from the chest, elbow extended to the side, adding a little spin with the thumb, almost like throwing a Frisbee. Many beginners, frequently women, dip and bob up to throw and then release the dart with a little up-kick of one leg, like a starlet kissing Clark Gable in an old movie. Experts warn against it, but freely concede that a fine West Coast player, male, wins tournaments with precisely such a throw. One player takes two or three little aiming pokes at the board before throwing; another simply leans out and launches. Some must warm up; others cannot. Some practice; others don't. Rob White of Scotland throws with a pipe clenched in his teeth, George Linton of England prefers to play in his hat and overcoat, and the American Scott Tufts says, "I shoot in thermal underwear no matter what."

The average players, like weekend golfers, watch the superstars and remark upon their styles, mannerisms, and personalities, comment admiringly on their successful unorthodoxies and smirk at their unsuccessful ones. And then try to emulate those they admire most.

Yet many of the very finest players (Theide, Virachkul, Hitchcock come to mind) appear to have no "style" at all. Like the best of contemporary architecture, their game is refined, the structure explaining itself, form following function. Hypothesis: The more filigree and gingerbread in a player's game, the greater the chance for error.

In a sense the entire dart game is a single act, complete in itself, all of a piece. But for covenience it can be dismantled into steps and categories and laid out on a table for examination. The player's job is to put it all back together.

STANCE

You can stand any way you like so long as it is behind the throwing line, which means you must experiment and make a decision. English players tend to place themselves with both feet at the hockey, nearly foursquare to the board and quite stolidly erect, like Tom Barrett. Americans by and large have adopted a stance more in keeping with their forward-looking image of themselves, placing one foot (the one matching the throwing arm) forward with much weight on it, turning partly toward the board and leaning slightly forward, or in some cases (like Daniels, for example) quite far forward.

The rules allow either, the stolid erect or the alert leaning posture, and each has obvious advantages. Leaning gains a few inches of range, which helps, and standing upright lends stability, which also helps. It probably evens out in the end.

Some experts counsel that once the feet are planted at the line they should not be moved until the throw is completed, but others say there are times when they must be. Occasionally the spot you want is masked by a previous dart, and a half-step one way or the other can bring it into view. Daniels, for example, tacks as much as three feet back and forth, now far to one side when shooting a double, now in the middle and lined up for the 20s. Doing this means an interruption of concentration, however, and new input of range and angle. It takes a good player to do it without loss of rhythm.

Remember that this is a delicate business, the darts are small, the distance short, the target tiny, and the minutest change in the way you stand has a direct bearing on the success of the shot. The theme should be consistency in all things, including the stance, because the more you can do instinctively the less you have to think about. It is worth a day's practice session just to learn your own best stance, experimenting until you find one in which you feel composed, at ease, so that the throw itself is calm and comfortable. Common errors include swaying, lunging, dipping, raising the heels when throwing, leaning off balance, moving the head or body. Essentially these are mistakes of insecurity, attempts to compensate for something the unconscious (or the half-conscious, or the body) tells you is not right.

As in life, seek a firm serenity.

GRIP

Conrad Daniels told me that varying your dart grip a fraction of an inch can throw the dart six to eight inches off the mark, and I didn't believe him. Looking for proof one way or the other, I tried a grip experiment.

I sought carefully for what I felt was the best grip for me and my darts, and then using that grip I threw twenty-one darts at the bull. Then I varied the grip by moving one finger one-eighth of an inch, and threw twenty-one more darts at the bull.

And now I believe Daniels.

The first time, using the best of all possible grips, I hit the bull six times, and ten more darts were within an inch of it.

The second time, using the slightly altered grip, I hit the bull only once, and only seven darts were within an inch.

Of course this was most unscientific. I may have concentrated better, tried harder, the first time. Or felt more confident with a grip I was used to. But the difference was very dramatic and it doesn't really matter how it came about—because the experiment worked. I am convinced.

While the grip has to vary with the player, there are a few rules or principles. Generally, the more finger area touching the dart the better, as it lends control. A single-finger-and-thumb grip allows wobble, like trying to sit on a chair that has only two legs. Add another finger and the grip is more secure, a kind of tripod. Some players place their fingers at an angle across the barrel, fingertips toward the nose (of the dart) instead of at right angles to the barrel. This gives them a greater area of touch. Some even rest their third finger lightly on the point to steady it. The wrist is usually cocked loosely backward, then extended or straightened near the end of the throw—almost the way an *atlatl* assists a spear throw.

Again, consistency is the main thing, and for the same reasons. Unlike bowling balls, darts have no clues to suggest where the fingers should go. Conrad Daniels felt so strongly about this that he used to have two little pieces of Scotch tape on his darts to indicate finger positions. Daniels doesn't need those any more.

THROW

Stance and grip established, you must now aim and throw. The aiming process seems to happen less in the hand and the dart than in the eye, brain, and ganglia. Aiming a dart is something you do *as* you throw it, not before: It is active, not passive.

"It's not like sighting a gun," Daniels says, "it's like guiding a basketball."

Throwing a dart is a natural act, a graceful extension of the arm, a follow-through, perhaps with a straightening of the wrist at the end to add power for a flat trajectory, a quick opening flick of the fingers that allows the dart to go on its way.

"It's not a push action, it's a flow," says a top player.

The upper arm is at right angles to the body, and stays that way. Most of the action comes from the lower arm and wrist. Good players don't jerk, heave, plunge toward the target; they simply uncoil with enough smooth energy to ensure a flat flight path, and they have confidence. It is often a lack of confidence that embellishes a perfectly good simple style with useless and interruptive gaudy flourishes.

The English and the Americans tend to differ in throwing styles as well as stance. English players often throw a rhythmic set of three darts fairly quickly, so that they either get three good shots or three bad ones. Americans will more often stop themselves to let the tension drain away after a poor shot and create a new starting situation.

And once again, consistency is the key. Bring the dart to the same place each time, the eye, ear, nose, throat, shoulder—whatever feels right—and use the same motion for the throw. Theide throws from the chin, Daniels from the eye, but always in the same way.

PRACTICE

Many games are loose enough to absorb the occasional error, to allow mistakes and comebacks, but the classic game of 301 is less merciful. Unless each error of yours is matched by an equal mistake of your opponent's, you can never win.

Which means practice.

Some very good players never practice at all, or say they don't. But they play so much they do not need to. An hour a day is what most recommend, though the figure is arbitrary and a few go quite a lot further: "If you know anybody who wants to be a good darts shooter—tell him to get laid off and start hanging around in bars all day with no money. Pretty soon he'll get good."

Hazard is endemic to this approach: wallet bruises, liver damage, matrimonial strife. Even the most innocent practice carried to extremes can be dangerous. From leaning on one leg too long you may get dart knee. From throwing too long, dart arm—analogous to tennis elbow or Frisbee finger. One New Yorker developed arthritis in his right foot—from darts, they say—and Bob Theide has had two operations for removal of foot calluses.

Naturally, moderation is wise, but practice grooves your game so that you can play with the body instead of the mind, which is too complex an instrument to be allowed to muddy up the physical portion of the game. It will also be rather busy with the mental portion, about which more later. Practice tends to pare away those nonessential curlicues of style that interfere with throwing simple straight darts. It helps you memorize the board, improving rhythm. The more darts you throw, the less important each single dart seems, reducing tension. Practice is also a lot of fun.

Simply throwing random darts for an hour helps very little, however; you need discipline, direction, even perhaps a planned program.

One of the goals of practice is to develop a rhythmic toss: You want to be able to throw a dart with ease, then move on to throw the rest with no jerky interruption. Some of this happens in the mind. You have to know beforehand what number to throw for next, and be able to find it without having to pause and search. Somehow the body/mind makes small adjustments and corrections automatically, retaining and filing all the tiny computations of sight, weight, distance, angle, power, and cranking them into the next shot the way a fire-control computer aims a ship's big guns. If you switch off the computer—pause to think— you have erased all that data and when it has faded from the display panel you have to start all over again. Now and then you will want to do this deliberately, as when a dart blocks the target and you must move to see it, or when you have gotten into a snit and need to relax. But usually it is best for the beat to go on.

One good practice routine for rhythm is the three-number call. Simply think of three numbers, and then throw for them in order in as fluid a series as you can. Relax, don't rush, but don't pause. It will improve your ability to switch numbers in mid-throw.

Equally important is throwing tight groupings. Doing so means precision and consistency. A good way to practice for it is to throw one dart at any number, then try to place two following darts right beside it. The first serves as a goal, like the pin in golf.

An excellent practice regimen, and probably the most common, is throwing Round the Clock. Beginners should start with singles: Try to hit each wedge in numerical order, 1 through 20 and then bull, always keeping a rhythm. Perfect score is 21 darts to finish. As you improve, move up to throwing doubles and triples. Tom Barrett, when at the top of his form, can hit any double or triple with a maximum of two darts, and hit the 50 with a maximum of three.

The best practice—nothing will pull your game up quicker—is to play with someone who is better than you are.

One secret of helpful practice is not to simply throw darts, but to actually, truly, concentrate very hard as if each throw were game point in a match against Conrad Daniels. And perfect—in Saul Bellow's phrase, "an intensification of vision."

HEAD STUFF

The brain is strange terrain.

Lorna Croft looks down and sees Olly's darts in her hand. "Oh!" she blurts, "I'd better put these away, otherwise I'll be accused of getting them all hot."

Ed McDevitt: "Once you get that dart touch you don't want to hold a cold beer, a hot cigarette—you don't want to hold anything but a dart."

Adele Nutter: "Don't defile that hand. I even learned how to write on the blackboard with my left hand. I was really eccentric about it. And I used to always have to wear a black shirt."

Conrad Daniels: "Your feet get tired. I do a lot of running to stay in shape. I wear support stockings when I play. I wear the same shoes for tournaments. Tennis shoes are bad; they create a roll. I wear hard shoes. Consistency is important too—don't wear tennis shoes one time and cordovans the next. It all affects the play. Shirts in or out, long sleeves or short sleeves, a heavy belt buckle or no belt. It all affects the darts. Three-beer players should play with three beers. I've seen good dart players play one game with low heels and another with high heels—you know, that will add two inches to a person's game. If I'm staying at a hotel I'll go lie down for an hour, shower, and change my clothes. Except for my shoes."

Tony Wood: "Alan Evans is very superstitious. He hates to play on the 13th, and he's lost two major tournaments on that date. Jean Smith, a top woman player from Bristol, plays in a red beret and throws it into the air when she wins."

Charlie Young: "If I've shot well the first day of a tournament I don't change clothes. The cigarettes in my shirt pocket have to be a certain way."

Ray Fischer: "I can't wear a hat. The dart keeps tipping the brim. Dart players are finicky. You get fussy up there. I'm standing at the line and if there's something under my feet—a piece of paper, whatever—I have to move it. Everything has to be just right."

Nobody doubts that the mind and emotions are a potent component in any athletic performance, and darts players can keep up with anyone as they speak of concentration, composure, confidence, serenity, mental preparation, psyching oneself up (or down, or occasionally even out). Most can offer one or two concrete suggestions:

Daniels: "Don't run to the dartboard immediately; sit down and have a couple of drinks. Maintain a level of relaxation."

Scheerbaum: "It's a lot mental. Most of the time I don't think of who I am playing or even watch the game. I just play my darts. I never let it enter my head at all."

Virachkul: "Concentration is the whole thing—and being ready to lose and not let it take the heart away from you."

Ennis: "Temperament."

Gopar: "I think having a positive attitude is very important.

Don't feel that just because you're up against a good player that you're going to lose. So many times you can surprise yourself by winning. You might call it luck, but I'd almost call it pure fear— you want to win so bad that you can."

You can see from Gopar's remarks how complex and paradoxical this is—"pure fear" being equated with "a positive attitude." A queer psychology sometimes operates, and the only way to overcome this is to expect it and think twice. The late Tom Bertles, a New York waiter who called himself a "dart doctor," said: "Sometimes beginners instead of looking at what they want, say a double 20, lack confidence and look all around at what they'll get if they miss." Presumably, this is a foible that can be overcome with the conscious mind. Some, like the death wish of the chronic loser, probably can't.

There are at least two schools of thought as to what concentration in sports really is. One of them sees it as a stern, controlling, take-charge, Western sort of mind-control force: You WILL stare at that bull's-eye, you WILL throw straight for it, you WILL hit it. The idea is steely and fierce, a conscious focusing of attention—a matter of will and want, mind over matter. Jargonizing, it is goal-oriented.

On the other hand is Zen, or an approximation of it. The Zen master who taught Eugen Herrigel, author of the classic *Zen in the Art of Archery*, told him ". . . the right art is purposeless, aimless! What stands in your way is that you have too much willful will." (It is Queen Farah's pronouncement couched in other language.)

These two schools hardly sound the same, but I have a feeling they are really different *sides* of the same thing: more Ying and Yang. It is not surprising to me that a lot of American darts players have lately become enamored of yoga and transcendental meditation as well as booze (transcendental medication?).

For players of a certain temperament, the mystics may be onto something. One, named Mike Murphy, says, "When the golfer can visualize and execute his shot in a moment of high clarity, the ball rides the energy streamer right up to the green." The quarterback John Brodie spoke of the same thing: "The player can't be worrying about the past or the future or the crowd or some other extraneous event. He must be able to respond in the here and now; I believe we all have this naturally. Maybe we lose it as we grow up. At times I experience a kind of clarity that I've never seen described in any football story; sometimes things seem to slow way down as if everyone were moving in slow motion. It seems as if I have all the time in the world to watch the receivers run their patterns, and yet I know the defensive line is coming at me just as fast as ever, and yet the whole thing seems like a movie or a dance in slow motion. It's beautiful."

When darts went to Japan, Zen darts instructors sprang up overnight. Zen players became so good that one American Air Force club banned them from play: they never lost.

Here is what Zen darts instructor Ko Ishizaka told *Darts World* magazine:

"Darts is as simple as walking or weighing a dart in your hands. Do not think of every individual movement during your game. Allow your actions to come naturally. You must wipe them clean of all emotion—all anxiety, all tension, all will to win—and let the muscles do their job. You cannot possibly miss that board when your dart flies through the air. The human body is a precision instrument. But there are hundreds of interlocking muscles, and they can exert their utmost power only when there is no unnatural strain anywhere, allowing the muscles to work in harmonious coordination. The most important element of each dart game is not the form or the arm swing, but the things which do not take any form—such as breathing, mental attitude, and muscle preparation. The forward swing begins in the toes and is transmitted through the legs and the body to the arm. As the arm moves forward let the dart absorb the acceleration inherent in any moving object. This acceleration reaches its peak after the dart is released from the hand. At that moment the wrist uncocks with directional guidance . . . the acceleration built up for the dart by the hand is not willed. The board is simply in the path of the true-aimed dart. The Zen mind is not in any way concerned with actually striking the board; in truth there should be no mental wish to hit the board at all; this only causes strain. This does not mean that the player is unaware of the board or the darts; the Zen mind within is completely absorbed in the harmonious movement of the muscles . . . whether or not the dart in fact strikes the board is virtually decided before the dart is raised. Your Zen mind is mentally fused with the board, yet remains detached. Although you are carefully aware of the board in your sights, your mind is not moved or influenced by it. The board is not to be hit by the dart—the dart is only to be propelled on its predetermined way by the player's spirit, or soul, in harmony with the total environment."

This is heady stuff, but even hard-headed Occidentals are beginning to perceive a power in it. If Zennis works, maybe Zarts does too.

TACTICS

To play 301 well you have to understand the game itself, the board it is played on, and the numerical combinations and probabilities involved in playing it.

The rules of the game are simple. Any beginner can grasp them in a minute or two, go on to play, surely have fun, and maybe even win. It is later that complexities exfoliate and the challenge becomes clearer: opportunities to plan ahead, time to prepare in advance for certain breaks and perhaps to make breaks, probabilities and percentages to be taken advantage of.

In any game of 301 there are three distinct phases.

1. Doubling-in—hitting the initial double that allows you to play.

2. Earning points as quickly as possible—reducing your score to a low enough even number so that you can double-out.

3. The end game—doubling-out and all that leads to it.

From this you can see that the most important physical skill is being able to hit a double.

Mentally, it is knowing which double to hit.

DOUBLING-IN

Nothing you do in 301 has meaning until you have first hit a double—placed a dart somewhere, anywhere, in the outer ring. Rules permit doubling-in on the double bull, but it's a skimpy target and best left to experts and the lucky. Hitting a double is not easy and entire games have been played while one mortified player stood there trying to do it; this is called getting white-washed, possibly because some people in this situation tend to turn a little pale.

All the doubles are the same size, and every player has favorite numbers to throw at, and this is a consideration when starting a game. But a little thought suggests some doubles are better than others: those at the sides of the board. The throwing arm moves on a vertical plane, so that if you are lined up with a side double the main consideration is merely when to let go of the dart. On the sides there is a vast margin for error. Shooting for the double 6, you can throw a little high and still luck into double 13, or a little low and hit double 10. Sometimes a kiss shot helps. Say you have placed one dart just to the right of double 6. You might throw the second straight at the dart, bouncing it off the dart and into the double. This can work more often than you think, even for mediocre players.

Some good players prefer to double-in at the double-16 and double-8 area, since the strategies of the game make this a frequently sought segment of the dartboard. More about this later, but keep it in mind.

SCORING HIGH

Imagine that you have aimed for double 6 and lucked into the double 10. You are in the game with 20 points, giving you a score of 281. Your job now is to pile up points fast.

A moment's study of the dartboard reveals a Luciferian deployment of numbers. All the high ones have been flanked by some sly fallen angel with *low* ones, which means the player is penalized for an ambitious throw that misses. You can see this most clearly in the 20—and the 1 and 5 that flank it like sand traps beside a golf green.

Yet the bull, which looks tempting, is also a problem. If you threw double bulls, which is very difficult, you'd get only 150 points. Three triple 20s, a larger target, yields 180. In fact, three triple anything over 17 is better pointwise than three bulls.

If you are a very good player and sure of yourself, the best place for scoring high is the triple 20, the highest on the board. But the less sure shot may do better elsewhere. For such a player the highest average scores may be found in the lower left quadrant, the area between 11 and 19. The 19 is only one point less than 20, but it is flanked with higher numbers than the 20. Also, some people feel more comfortable working the bottom of the board.

END GAME

The real challenge in 301 is the end game, in which tactics and skill have brought the player to a point where he can double-out. There is a good deal of excitement in the uncertainty of the final double, and a rare exhilaration in achieving it first to win.

Cartoon interlude: Two Roman soldiers in plumed helmets are standing in a pub playing darts. One of them throws, turns to the other, says: "What's LXVII from CCCI?"

There are two ways of playing out the end game. The first is simply to keep on chucking darts until you reach a small, manageable double number, say double 5, and then try for that. If you miss, then adapt to whatever new situation presents itself. Of necessity, this is the way beginners play, and it is great fun.

The other way is the Way of the Pro, and it is extremely challenging. And surprisingly difficult.

Between any two equally talented shooters what makes the

crucial difference is something dartists call "knowing your numbers" or "learning to count." They are fond of saying, "There are a lot of no-count dart players around."

The best players have reams of numerical combinations committed to memory, and swatches of alternatives in case they miss their first choice. By the time an expert reaches a score of 160 or so, he is already planning his outshot. Here, for example, is the path one top shooter would take to the finish, in three darts, if he had 129 left. With scarcely a thought he would throw for triple 19 with his first dart. If he hit it, he'd be left with 72. He would throw for double 18 with his second, leaving 36—double 18. On his third, he would throw another double 18 to finish.

You can see how difficult that is. For one thing, a miss at any point interrupts his entire strategy. For another, he is trying, with his second and third darts, to place *two* darts side by side in the same double—no easy feat.

So suppose he misses.

Again without thought (or so he says), he knows what to do. If he misses the triple 19 and hits the single 19, he will immediately try to throw a triple 20 and then a double bull to finish.

It is possible, for an expert, to make a three-dart out when his score is still as high as 170. It is not easy, though, and it is not done often.

But three-dart outs from 170 or even from 129 are something of a daydream for the novice. For us, real opportunities do not appear until the score is well below 100.

Because learning all of this takes time—and for some of us, less dedicated than others, may be impossible anyway—number-minded folk have compiled charts that tell how to throw winning darts. One of these is reproduced here. It shows the shortest distance between two points—your present score, and a good outshot. Keep in mind, however, that the chart shows only some possibilities out of many; even the experts don't agree on the question of the perfect outshot. There are lots of other charts to try.

TIPS AND STRATEGIES FOR WINNING

WINNING COMBINATIONS CHART

170—t20, t20, ×B	136—t20, t20, ×8	113—t19, 16, ×20
167—t19, t20, ×B	135—t19, t14, ×18	113—t19, t8, ×16
164—t19, t19, ×B	134—t20, t14, ×16	113—19, t18, ×20
161—t19, t18, ×B	133—t19, t12, ×20	112—t20, 20, ×16
161—t20, t17, ×B	132—t20, t12, ×18	112—t18, t14, ×8
160—t20, t20, ×20	131—t19, t14, ×16	112—18, t18, ×20
158—t20, t20, ×19	130—t20, t18, ×8	111—t19, 18, ×18
157—t19, t20, ×20	129—t19, t12, ×18	110—t20, ×B
156—t20, t20, ×18	128—t20, 18, ×B	110—20, t18, ×18
155—t19, t20, ×19	128—t20, t20, ×4	109—t19, 20, ×16
154—t18, t20, ×20	128—t20, t12, ×16	109—19, t18, ×18
153—t19, t20, ×18	127—t19, t18, ×8	108—t20, 8, ×20
152—t20, t20, ×16	126—t20, t10, ×18	108—t20, 16, ×16
151—t20, t17, ×20	125—t19, t20, ×4	108—20, t16, ×20
151—t19, t18, ×20	124—t20, t16, ×8	107—t19, ×B
150—t20, t18, ×18	123—t19, t10, ×18	107—t17, 16, ×20
149—t19, t20, ×16	122—t20, t10, ×16	107—t16, 19, ×20
148—t20, t16, ×20	121—t19, t16, ×8	107—t18, 17, ×18
147—t19, t18, ×18	120—t20, 20, ×20	106—t20, 6, ×20
147—t20, t17, ×18	119—t19, t10, ×16	106—t20, 10, ×18
146—t20, t18, ×16	119—19, t20, ×20	105—t19, 8, ×20
145—t19, t16, ×20	118—t20, 18, ×20	105—t19, 16, ×16
145—t17, t18, ×20	118—20, t20, ×19	104—t18, ×B
144—t20, t16, ×18	117—t19, 20, ×20	104—t18, 18, ×16
143—t19, t18, ×16	117—19, t20, ×19	104—t20, 4, ×20
143—t17, t20, ×16	116—t20, 16, ×20	103—t19, 6 ×20
142—t20, t14, ×20	116—20, t20, ×18	103—t19, 10, ×18
141—t17, t14, ×20	115—t19, 18, ×20	102—t20, 6, ×18
141—t19, t16, ×18	115—19, t20, ×18	102—t20, 10, ×16
140—t20, t16, ×16	114—t20, 18, ×18	101—t19, 12, ×16
139—t19, t16, ×16	114—t20, 14, ×20	101—t16, 17, ×18
138—t20, t14, ×20	114—20, t18, ×20	101—t20, 17, ×12
137—t19, t16, ×16	114—t18, 20, ×20	100—t20, ×20

THREE IN A BED

99—t19, 10, ×16	75—t17, ×12	56—16, ×20
98—t20, ×19	74—t14, ×16	56—t8, ×16
98—t16, ×B	74—14, 20, ×20	56—t16, ×4
97—t19, ×20	73—t19, ×8	55—15, ×20
96—t20, ×18	73—t11, ×20	54—18, ×18
95—t19, ×19	72—t12, ×18	54—14, ×20
94—t18, ×20	72—t20, ×6	53—13, ×20
93—t19, ×18	72—t16, ×12	53—17, ×18
92—t20, ×16	71—t13, ×16	52—12, ×20
91—t17, ×20	70—t18, ×8	52—20, ×16
90—t18, ×18	70—18, 12, ×20	51—19, ×16
89—t19, ×16	69—t11, ×18	50—×B
88—t16, ×20	69—t19, ×6	50—18, ×16
87—t17, ×18	69—19, ×B	49—17, ×16
86—t18, ×16	68—t20, ×4	49—t11, ×8
85—t15, ×20	68—18, ×B	49—11, ×19
84—t20, ×12	67—t17, ×8	48—8, ×20
84—t16, ×18	67—17, ×B	48—16, ×16
84—16, t20, ×4	66—t10, ×18	47—15, ×16
83—t17, ×16	65—t11, ×16	46—6, ×20
82—t14, ×20	65—t19, ×4	46—10, ×18
81—t19, ×12	64—t20, ×2	45—13, ×16
81—19, t10, ×16	64—t16, ×8	45—5, ×20
80—t16, ×16	63—t9, ×18	44—4, ×20
80—16, t8, ×20	62—t10, ×16	44—18, ×13
80—t20, ×20	61—t15, ×8	43—11, ×16
79—t17, ×14	61—15, 6, ×20	43—3, ×20
79—17, t10, ×16	61—B, ×18	42—6, ×18
78—t18, ×12	61—t7, ×20	42—10, ×16
78—t14, ×18	60—20, ×20	41—9, ×16
77—t19, ×10	59—19, ×20	41—1, ×20
76—t20, ×8	58—18, ×20	40—×20
75—t13, ×18	57—17, ×20	

Many good players employ these charts, at least until they have mastered the numbers, and it is nothing to be ashamed of. For one thing, the chart hardly solves all the problems. You still have to throw the dart where it tells you to, which is never easy.

Sometimes the novice is tempted to skip these ambitious high-number shots and placidly go on throwing 19s and 20s till his score drops to a point where he can see what's going on. That does seem more appealing, sometimes, than risking a triple-shot you doubt you can make. But the experts counsel against such a slack game and they are right, if only for reasons of aesthetic discipline, of playing the game for its perfect beauty. Even if you miss that impossible triple you'll hit *something*, and those points count too. And of course you might hit it. Finally, if you don't go for the difficult, demanding, satisfying, effective, *best* shot, and your opponent does, you will lose a lot more games than you will win. Darts is just for fun, of course, but between winning and losing, winning is better.

As long as your score remains above 100 or so you can throw at any old number without doing much damage, just accumulating points, but when the game has narrowed toward its end much more precision is called for. Individual players have a variety of schemes and plots; here is some general theory.

The first thing to do is make your score even as early as possible, and try to keep it even. This is important because if you are stuck with an odd-numbered score at the critical final stage of the game, you will have to waste at least one dart just to even up. In close games, such profligacy can cost all.

You are ready to double-out when your score is even and low enough so that one dart into a double will reduce it to zero. Fifty (double bull) is the highest possible outshot; otherwise you can double-out only after you have 40 or less. By looking at the board and thinking in numbers, you can begin devising a rudimentary strategy.

You notice for instance that it is smart to plan ahead so that you won't be trying to double-out on an odd-number segment, because that is chancy and potentially wasteful. Say you have allowed yourself to end up with 30 points—a double 15. This is a perfectly good place to be—if you can hit the double 15. But if you miss a little inside, hitting the single 15, then your are stuck with 15 points left. It is an odd number, and you have to waste a dart to even up again—just what you've been avoiding all along. So a lesson can be drawn. Try to land on an even-numbered double.

This reasoning can be carried further. If even doubles are better than odd doubles, are some even doubles better than others? Yes, some are. The ideal one is 32—double 16. Virtually all fine players have this number seared into their brains and plan how they will reach it a hundred points ahead of time.

The enchanting thing about 32 is that it can be split by accident no fewer than five times without necessitating a wasted dart to even up. No other number can make this claim. If you shoot for double 16 and hit single 16, you would simply go on and shoot for double 8. If you miss and hit the single 8 instead, simply go on to shoot double 4, and so on. You can do that five times, which makes 32 the nearest thing to magic the game can boast.

Demi-magical is the number 40, which on the same theory is a good second choice. If you throw for double 20 and miss inside, you are left with double 10; miss that and it is double 5. But that is as far as it goes. You get three chances and then are left with 5 (odd) points and have to squander a dart to get even.

It is a bit of luck, also, that both 20 and 16 are numbers used in American cricket, so players who enjoy that game are comfortable shooting at them.

Some experts recommend even higher numbers to strive for—numbers that in effect are way stations on the route to 32 or 40 and place you in a better potential scoring position more quickly. Try, for instance, to bring your score to 80, then shoot double 20, then double 20 again to finish. This is a good one because if you miss and hit only a single 20, you are still even, you can hit another single 20, then the double, and still finish neatly. Note that this is precisely the same as going for the 40; you are just looking for it earlier. Similarly with 64 and 48. You can look for these early too. If you have 48 you can shoot 16, giving you 32, and then proceed as before. With 64 shoot either double 16, then double 16 again, or shoot two single 16s (by accident or deliberately, to keep the doubles ring open for the finishing shot), and then double 16.

Bear in mind that these are only a few possibilities and in any given situation the brilliant out-shot you attempt might be disdained by another player with a different notion of brilliance.

Sometimes even the negative aspects of the game can be turned to advantage. Take the bust for example. If you bust, or throw more points than you have left, you must cease throwing and your score reverts to what it was at the start of the throw. Usually that hurts. But sometimes it can be used to help.

For instance: You have 16 left and you try for it. But instead of hitting the double 8, or even the tidy single 8 that would have left you even, you hit a sloppy 13. You have 3 points left. That gives you only one option if you want to play it: Hit a 1, then a double 1. You could do that, and many players would. But maybe you have only one dart left. Or maybe you have got used to the 32-16-etc. combination and would prefer to shoot for it. You could then deliberately bust by throwing a high number, leaving yourself back at 16 for the next throw.

These are the basics of the game. All of it helps, but no matter how good you get you will still miss now and then. I have seen no less a superstar than Conrad Daniels take careful aim at the 20 and throw a 7, which is about as bad a shot as it is possible to make. Yet even that works both ways. Sometimes, no matter how you throw it, a dart is simply going to land in the right place as if by itself, and that is one of the best moments in the game. It never guarantees you will win, but it lets you imagine that you might next time.

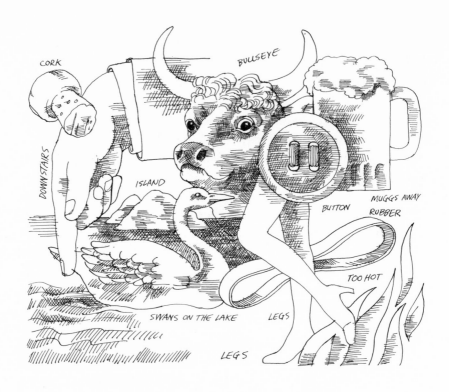

GLOSSARY
THE SLANGUAGE OF DARTS

The language of darts is English, though a curiously specialized hybrid combining Cockney rhyming slang, metaphor, and the sometimes exotic imagery that turns up in the conversation of the sociable people who spend a lot of time in bars. In darts, there is a formal name for every part and act, and a slang name for most of them as well. The slanguage is much more frequently and densely used in England, but when the game found itself in America some of the talk had come along too. A bit of it, such as the word "cork" for bull's-eye, is more commonly used here than abroad.

If you set serious philosophy aside, in daily life the names of things are part of their essence, and anyone who wants to understand the ambience of the darts scene should be familiar with its tongue. You may have noticed that although this book is intended to touch on every important aspect of the game, from its origins to its recent boom, remarkably little of this odd lingo has been used in doing so: The language isn't a necessary part of the game. You can play without knowing any of it, and play very well, but it is not as much fun, and you can't intimidate a darts-illiterate opponent with a knowing mutter of "fevvers" when he's got 33 points left. That's got to count for something. And if you know the talk, when you lose you've got euphemisms all prepared to describe your humiliating condition a bit less frankly.

Note, though, that some of these words are name-calling words. When you use them on an opponent the tone should be sympathetic, not derisive. That's part of the game too.

Annie's room—the number 1.

Arrow—a dart.

Away—started; in 301, when a player has doubled-in. Usually combined with the appropriate number, as in "12 away," when the player has hit double 6.

Bag o' nuts—the number 45.

Bed—a portion of the board, usually a given double or triple area, as in "three in a bed," *q.v.*

Bed and breakfast—the number 26. A long time ago in England a bed and breakfast in an inn could be had for 2/6d.: two shillings and sixpence. In darts, used to refer to 20, 5, and 1, never to double 13. Bed and breakfast is what you get when trying to throw three darts into the 20, get one, and miss once to each side.

Bill Harvey—the number 100; also called a "ton."

Brush—whitewash, *q.v.*

Bull—bull's-eye.

Bung—bull's-eye.

Bunghole—bull's-eye.

Bust—to score more points than you need, or one less, when shooting for a final double. You've then "bust," "busted," or "gone bust," and your score reverts to what it was before the throw began.

Button—bull's-eye.

Cane—to defeat badly, as in "He was caned off the board." Employed, no doubt, mainly by old public-school boys. A cane is also a shaft made of willow or split bamboo.

Chucker—a mediocre, maladroit, absentminded, or uncommitted darts player; a duffer.

Clickety-click—the number 66.

Clock—a dartboard.

Come out—stop throwing, you've busted.

Connaught Rangers—the number 88.

Cork—bull's-eye. Often used in the United States.

Crack—what you have to do when you have an odd number left: Crack it by hitting another odd number bringing your score even for the outshot. Also: rip, split.

Dart—the pointed, feathered object you throw; the act of throwing it.

Darts—more than one of the above; the name of the game.

" 'Darts"—abbreviated form of the expression "Good darts," a compliment on a good throw.

Dinky doo—the number 22.

Doctor's favorite—the number 9.

Dosser—the bull's-eye.

Double-in—the act of throwing the first double in a —01 game that allows your scores to count.

Double-out—the act of throwing the final double in a —01 game.

Downstairs—the lower half of the board.

Dry wipe—what it's called when a player wins the first two legs of a three-leg game, thus shutting out his opponent and winning.

Feathers—the number 33.

Fevvers—the number 33. From a Cockney saying, "Firty-free fousand fevvers on a frush's froat."

Fish shop—the number 22.

Fried fish—the number 22.

Front room—a close game. The saying goes, "It's like our front room; there's nothing in it." I don't understand this exactly, but that's what they say.

Game shot—uttered after a player doubles-out and wins; also, office, bingo, house, domino.

Garden gates—the number 88.

Get in—to double-in and begin the game.

Get on—ditto; as in to "get on the board."

Get out—to double-out; as "He got out on double bull."

Golden gate(s)—the number 88.

"Good darts"—a compliment: nice throwing.

Half a crown, or 'arf a crown—the number 26.

Hard cheddar—too bad; nice try; tuff darts.

Hard cheese—same as above.

Heinz—the number 57.

Hockey—the line from which darts are thrown. It should be three feet long. The standard distance in international play is eight feet.

Hops—remark to loser that it is his obligation to buy a round of drinks.

Island—the actual playing surface of the board, the area inside the outer doubles wire. "Off the island" is where you go if a dart falls outside it.

Kelly's eye—the number 1.

Key to the door—the number 21.

Leg—one of the (usually three) complete games, from double-in to double-out, that often make up a game or match in competition play.

Leg to leg—the situation in which each side has won one leg and a third must be played to determine the winner.

Legs—the number 11.

Level pegging—the situation in which the opponents are scoring about equally: a close game.

Lord Nelson—the number 111.

Madhouse—the double 1; also, the situation in which two players have come to the point where they are both shooting at the double 1 as a finish.

Married man's side—the left side of the board.

Middle for diddle—the situation in which, before a game, each player throws a single dart for the bull: closest one chooses the game and whether he will throw first or last.

Muggs away—said to loser of the previous game; means "You go first this time." Noel Williamson, a dart poet, prefers the expression, "Unfortunates away," which is one of the funniest things I've ever heard.

Muggs off—muggs away, q.v.

On your knees—said to a player who finds himself with a double 3 to shoot for; it is low on the board and difficult enough to justify prayer in the pious.

One and double—said to a player with 3 points; means "You need a single 1, then a double 1."

Over-trained—remark to player who is too hot, or trying too hard.

Oxo—zero.

Pug—bull's-eye.

Rip—crack, q.v.

Ripped it—what a player has done if, throwing for a double, he misses and leaves himself with an odd number; also, torn it.

Robin Hood—to throw a dart into the stern of an earlier one already in the board, which happens more frequently than might be expected. The second dart, as it is not in the face of the board, earns no score.

Rubber—the final leg of a three-leg game.

Skunked—whitewashed, q.v.

Spider—the metal web that divides segments on the board and

determines (regardless of coloration) the score earned by any dart.

Split—crack, *q.v.*

Sufferin'—as in "You're sufferin'." You either have a tough shot to make, or you've just narrowly missed one.

Sunset strip—the number 77.

Swans on the lake—the number 22.

Three in a bed—three darts in one number, usually a triple or double. Three in the triple 20 bed earns a ton-80, which is the dart player's hole in one.

Throw—a throw is three darts, tossed in sequence.

Tin hat—whitewash, *q.v.*

Ton—100 points.

Ton-40—140 points.

Ton-60—160 points.

Ton-80—180 points.

Too hot—you've thrown too many points and busted; stop throwing.

Top o' the house—double 20, which is at the very top of the board.

Top o' the shop—double 20.

Trombones—the number 76.

Tough darts, or tuff darts—nice try; too bad.

Two little ducks—the number 22.

Umbrellas—the number 77.

Up in Annie's room—the number 1.

Upstairs—the top half of the dartboard.

Wet feet—feet that have stepped over the hockey; foot fault.

Whitewash—the situation in which one player in a —01 game has completed the entire cycle and doubled-out, winning, before his opponent has even doubled-in.

You've been—a brusque way of saying "You've busted"; much like saying "You've had your chance and you blew it; step aside."

Varieties—the number 57.

Wrong bed—comment when a dart has gone into an undesired segment: "You missed." (Or "I missed.")

ABOUT THE AUTHOR

JACK MCCLINTOCK is a free-lance writer who lives with his wife in a bay-front house he built in Indian Rocks Beach, Florida. He has written for *Esquire, Playboy, Harper's, TV Guide, Saturday Review, Rolling Stone, Travel & Leisure, Book World, Bookletter, Harper's Weekly,* the *Mother Earth News, The New York Times* and the *Washington Post. The Book of Darts* is his first book. He has played darts for two years at a startling level of mediocrity. Currently he is trying to write country songs and magazine articles, and preparing to rebuild a 200-year-old log cabin in the mountains of Northeast Georgia or move to New York City.